# YAHVEH CHRIST,

OR,

# THE MEMORIAL NAME.

BY

ALEXANDER MAC WHORTER,

YALE UNIVERSITY.

WITH

INTRODUCTORY LETTER

BY

NATHANIEL W. TAYLOR, D. D.,

DWIGHT PROFESSOR OF DIDACTIC THEOLOGY,

YALE THEOLOGICAL SEMINARY.

BOSTON:

GOULD AND LINCOLN,

59 WASHINGTON STREET.

NEW YORK: SHELDON, BLAKEMAN & CO.

CINCINNATI: GEORGE S. BLANCHARD.

1857.

Electro-Stereotyped by
G. J. STILES & COMPANY,
23 Congress Street, Boston.

To

REV. SAMUEL DAVIDSON, D.D., LL.D.,

TO WHOSE SERVICES

IN THE CAUSE OF BIBLICAL LITERATURE,

ENGLAND

OWES A DEBT OF GRATITUDE,

THIS LITTLE VOLUME IS DEDICATED, AS

A TRIBUTE OF RESPECT

FROM

AMERICA.

# PREFACE.

THE following pages contain a popular presentation of Facts known hitherto, for the most part, only to Scholars.

Their momentous bearing upon the proper understanding of the Scriptures, especially of the Old Testament, will be acknowledged by all.

The name "Jehovah" is the grand central fact upon which the discussion turns.

It will be shown that this Name, having been deprived of its true vowels through a superstition of the Jews, is not "*Jehovah*," but YAHVEH; that it is not properly rendered "I am," but HE WHO WILL BE; that it is the Great Messianic Name of the Old Testament, and there represents the same Divine Person, who afterward appeared in the world's history under the name of CHRIST.*

* A paper entitled, "Jehovah; considered as a Memorial Name," prepared for scholars, with critical references, &c., &c., will be found in the Bibliotheca Sacra, Jan., 1857. Warren F. Draper, Andover, Mass. Trübner & Co., 12 Paternoster Row, London.

1*

An earnest attention is invited to the Historical Argument growing out of the relations of this Fact.

In the course of the discussion involving points confessedly dark to our Translators, their version has been spoken of as at fault.

It can hardly be supposed that the researches of scholars, for three centuries, have added nothing of value toward the elucidation of the Hebrew Scriptures,—nothing in the shape of new constructions and new facts, of which those wise and good men, had they lived in our day, would not eagerly have availed themselves in their work.

We are not, however, among those who would exchange the dear, familiar, old English Bible, for any thoroughly modern version. Its language is a consecrated tongue, and must always remain so.

The only improvement to be desired would be, the clearing up, so far as possible, of dark or doubtful passages, the rectification of known errors, and the arrangement of poetry and prose, as they stand in the Original.

Such a translation would give a new impulse to the study of the Old Testament, and would, we believe, hasten the time when "the earth shall be full of the *knowledge* of YAHVEH, as the waters cover the sea."

# CONTENTS.

## CHAPTER I.



## CHAPTER II.



## CHAPTER III.



## CHAPTER IV.

## CHAPTER V.



## CHAPTER VI.



## CHAPTER VII.



## CHAPTER VIII.

# INTRODUCTORY LETTER.

---

THE subject of this volume is one of great and universal interest to Christians,—especially as involving an important question between Trinitarians and Unitarians.

The argument is altogether new and original, and if valid, *proves* what many of the ablest theologians have believed, without resting their belief upon grounds so thoroughly and rigidly exegetical.

It raises a question to be met wherever the Bible is read, a question in respect to a fact, which it would seem, if not admitted, must at least be controverted.

If the view here taken is erroneous, it is too plausible to be passed over with indifference by the friends of truth;—if true, it is of unmeasured importance to the Church and to the world.

I only add, that just views of the moral government of God over this world since the Apostacy in Eden,—a government of Law and Grace, administered by Him who is the Seed promised to our first Parents,—the Jehovah Angel of the Patriarchs, the Messiah of the Jews, the Redeemer of the world, the King on the holy hill of Zion, and the Lamb in the midst of the Throne,—not only harmonize with, but almost seem to require, the import which the writer of this critique gives to the Hebrew word, יַהְוֶה (Yahveh).

NATH'L W. TAYLOR.

Yale College, *Oct.* 1, 1856.

# YAHVEH CHRIST.

---

## CHAPTER I.

### THE MEMORIAL NAME.

THERE is one fact of great moment, recorded in the history of God's intercourse with man, to which the Christian world has in all ages been strangely indifferent.

While questions and theories of comparatively trivial importance, and often of no practical bearing whatever, have occupied a prominent place in the minds of religious men, this great fact has been left unnoticed, and perhaps forgotten, in the sepulchre where centuries ago it was laid, wrapped up in its cerements of traditional superstition and false philosophy. And yet this fact — the MEMORIAL NAME, "Jehovah" — enfolds the whole doctrine of God in His relation to man, comprehends the work of Redemption, contains the law and the gospel, reaches back in its extended significance to the gates of Eden, and forward to the final coming of the Redeemer. It is this NAME, long buried, but now risen again in the light of modern investigation, to which we would restore the significance and glory of its ancient meaning.

It surely must be conceded, that if God has adopted any one word, and declared it to be His "*memorial name* to all generations," that word should be a theme of earnest inquiry. If any uncertainty hang over the true significance of its ancient forms, the uncertainty should be dispelled by diligent research. The whole Christian world — God's children, each one of whom has a personal concern in the meaning of this term — should compel the research, being assured that God would not commit the solemn act of mockery, of giving to man as a revelation and memorial, a word either uncertain or unmeaning.

If, then, in reply to an earnest prayer for some declaration of Himself by a name, we find a term given which is both uncertain and unmeaning, let us beware how we rob God of His glory, by allowing our ideas of Him to gather round a vague, and perhaps merely human conception.

Now God has given us a NAME as a MEMORIAL. It stands far back in the story of the ages, recounted by Moses and the prophets. We, in the full light of the glorious appearing of Jesus Christ,—we, who see in Him all the fullness of the Godhead, bodily,—give little heed to the name, or the memorial. What matters it to us? We have a more perfect revelation, and are content that God's ancient, chosen people should have invoked Him by the term XYZ, or any other expression of an unknown, or unknowable quantity. We are prone to think and to say, in our self-complacency: "They were not prepared for a complete revelation,"—"It was necessary to inspire them with awe and terror,"—and therefore, when Moses entreated the Lord for a NAME, by which he might justify to the children of Israel his mission as Deliverer, God answered: "Go tell them 'I am' hath sent you. This is my name forever, and this my '*memorial*' to all generations."

So at least we are told in Exodus 3: 14, where we find the phrase "I am" given as the interpreting synonym for "*Jehovah*." Our translators have also suppressed the name "Jehovah" in all cases where not, in their view, especially emphatic, and have given us instead, the inexpressive feudal title "Lord."

So far as our translation goes then, there is no reason why we should not substitute the English "I am," as an equivalent for "Lord," in almost every instance in which the latter occurs in the Old Testament. This is a perfectly valid test, and should such a rendering seem unmeaning or unworthy, in any connection in which it is thus made to stand, this fact, of itself, would afford a strong presumption that we have not arrived at the true significance of the term.

Let us apply this test to a passage in the

history of the Israelites, in which the name JEHOVAH is most emphatically set forth by God Himself, in connection with a promise of DELIVERANCE.

It was an occasion of great distress among that suffering people. Moses had come with a message of Deliverance from God, who had declared that with a strong arm He would free them from bondage. Pharaoh would not listen, but increased their tasks. Moses and Aaron, day by day, besought the Lord for the promised Deliverance; but it was still delayed. Burden after burden was added, till the heart of the people was sick. They accused Moses and Aaron of being the instigators of this additional cruelty. They refused to believe in the promised Deliverance. The faith of Moses himself began to waver, or at least, to wonder, at the delay in the fulfilment of the promise. Hear his almost reproachful language: "Lord, wherefore hast thou so evil entreated this people? Why is it that thou hast sent me? for since I came to Pharaoh to speak in thy name, he hath done evil unto this people; neither hast thou delivered thy people at all!"

Now let us consider the answer made to Moses in these circumstances. Let us remember, that God is a God of loving-kindness, and tender mercy; and that these were His own people, in deep distress — so deep, that "they hearkened not to Moses, for anguish of spirit and cruel bondage." Let us substitute the phrase "I am," carrying with it the meaning of "*self-existence*," for the term "Lord," or "Jehovah," wherever it occurs in the answering declaration, and see how much of meaning, or of comfort, it carries with it.

And God spake unto Moses, and said unto him: "I am the 'I AM,' and I appeared unto Abraham, unto Isaac, and unto Jacob, by the name of God Almighty (Hebrew, El Shaddai); but by my name 'I AM' was I not known unto them. * * * And I have also heard the groaning of the children of Israel, whom the Egyptians keep in bondage, and I have remembered my covenant; wherefore say unto the children of Israel, I am the 'I AM,' and I will bring you out from under the burdens of the Egyptians, and I will rid you out of their bondage, and I will redeem you with a stretched-out arm, and with great judgments, and I will take you to me for a people, and I will be to you a God, and ye shall *know* that I am the 'I AM,' your God, which bringeth you out from under the burdens of the Egyptians."

It is possible, doubtless, to surround this proclamation, as it is usually thought to be, of the majesty of God's Immutable Existence, with a halo of metaphysical glory. It is no doubt possible, to build upon it many truths concerning the natural attributes of the Creator, which are inseparable from Him in that relation. But, to those who are accustomed to this view, one or two questions may be put, for common sense to answer.

Does not such a proclamation seem *out of place*, in the circumstances?

If the fact of the *power* of God, to accomplish what he had promised, was the fact he wished to impress upon the Israelites, why was not the name *God Almighty* sufficient?

Is there not, on the face of the narrative, an implication of a greater difference in the significance of these names, than appears in our translation?

Is it not probable, also, that a name adopted under such circumstances, to be perpetuated as a *memorial* to all generations, would contain some fact revealed, or relation assumed by God, fitted to be remembered in the connection in which it was declared?

We should naturally expect that a *memorial* name, given in such a crisis, would express the relation in which God, the everlasting God, is brought *nearest* to His people; that it would represent those promises by which He was remembered with hope, through all the troubled times in which Zion was tossed with the tempest, and not comforted, save with the comfort of this MEMORIAL.

Finally, that it would be the name, or would represent the relation, by which in these last days, *we* should remember Him. There ought surely to be in our hearts some response to the exulting exclamation of David: "Extol him by the name of Yah!" and yet there is not, we will venture to say, among all the inheritors of

God's promises to-day, there is not one, who instinctively remembers Him by that name. The "I AM" of our Old Testament, is scarcely more to us now, as an expression of character, than the Brahm of the Hindoo, or the absolute "Sein" of the German philosopher. It is not the name of God now; it is not His memorial to *this* generation. God to us, is He who sent into the world our Lord Jesus Christ; or, nearer still, looking upon the man Christ Jesus, we exclaim: "Lo, this is our God! we have waited for Him!" But do we add, with the prophet: "This is *Jehovah!* we have waited for *Him*"?

What then has become of that ancient name, revealed for all time? and why is it not our memorial?

Out of these questions arise others. Have we the true rendering of this word? What is its history? What its significance?

In seeking to answer these questions, we would invite attention to some facts in the exegesis of this name, brought to light by modern scholarship. They are facts to which our translators had no access. It came to them simply as an *Ineffable Name*, without life, embalmed like a mummy in the superstition of the Jews,—a name unlawful to be uttered, or even written, with its true vowel points. And this name, thus unpronounced, and falsely written, had a traditional rendering, made out under the shadow of the Septuagint. The Platonizing school of Alexandria gave God's declaration, in Exodus 3 : 14, a Greek rendering, which may be translated "*the Being*" (self-existent), and so our translators give us "I am."

But, with respect to the proper pointing and literal rendering of the term "*Jehovah*," there is now among scholars, no difference of opinion. Let us look at the facts in the case, and then consider their bearing upon its true meaning.

The Hebrew, as all now know, had originally no vowel points; by which is meant, simply, that the words consisted of consonants, written without their vowels; these latter, in the record as it now stands, being represented by signs or points, added about five hundred years after

Christ, by certain Jewish Rabbins called "The Masorites."

These Masorites, in accordance with the Jewish superstition which did not allow them to pronounce this sacred name of God, gave the name which we call "Jehovah" the vowel signs or points taken from another name of God,—Adonai (Sovereign); and from these false vowels comes our pronunciation, "*Jehovah.*"

Two questions therefore arise:

First, What is the derivation?

Second, What is the true pointing, and consequent pronunciation, of the term rendered "Jehovah" in our Bibles?

The derivation was formerly a matter of contention. Many critics have striven to give it a source foreign to the Hebrew. It is useless now to record their futile labors. It is sufficient upon this point, to cite the remarkable change of opinion in Gesenius; the acknowledgment of which, is a fact creditable alike to the candor and scholarship of this great philologist, who is at once the founder and the master of Hebrew criticism.

By comparing his former manuals with the last edition of his Thesaurus, it will be seen, that while in the former he holds to an Egyptian or Greek derivation of this term, in the latter he says: "They lose their time and labor who endeavor to refer this name to a foreign origin."

Its true derivation is from HAVAH, the old root of the Hebrew verb "to be,"—a root-form so ancient as to have been dropped entirely from the prose of the Pentateuch, and retained only in the poetic form of the imperative; as in Gen. 27: 29, in the prophetic benediction of Isaac: HEVEH, "'*Be*' lord over thy brethren." The antiquity of this root-form will be again alluded to. This old root-form, HAVAH, found its equivalent in HAYAH, the ordinary form of the Hebrew verb "to be;" and it is in the third person singular, *future*, of this later verb, HAYAH ("to be"),—namely, in the form of its old future, YAHVEH,—that we find the true place and pointing of the word rendered "Jehovah" by our translators.

It is this form, YAHVEH (literally, *He will be*),

turned into the noun, or name, YAHVEH,—HE WHO WILL BE,—which God adopts as His name and memorial to all generations.

With respect to this exegesis of the term "*Jehovah*," so far as the interests of criticism are concerned, all scholars are now agreed. Gesenius and Ewald, on the side of philologists, Hengstenberg, Tholuck, Lutz, &c., &c., on the side of theologians, are united for once. They all agree in giving it the form YAHVEH, and the future tense, as its literal rendering. But more than this. God himself originally set forth the meaning of this great prophetic name, in the plainest terms.—Ex. 3: 14.

First, by the prophecy: "I WILL BE WHO I WILL BE."

Next, by the statement: "I, WHO WILL BE," hath sent you.

Finally, by giving as his memorial name, YAHVEH,—"HE WHO WILL BE."

That the force of these transitions may be appreciated, we will transcribe the passage in which they occur, the *future* being used in the original throughout.

"And God said unto Moses, I WILL BE WHO I WILL BE; and he said, Thus shalt thou say unto the children of Israel. I WHO WILL BE hath sent me unto you. And God said moreover unto Moses, Thus shalt thou say unto the children of Israel, HE WHO WILL BE, the God of your fathers, the God of Abraham, the God of Isaac, and the God of Jacob, hath sent me unto you. This is my name forever, and this is my memorial to all generations."

It may be remarked here, that these expressions are in the most absolute form of the future. It is not possible to the language to make them more so. To translate them by any other tense, is to depart from the original, as will appear more fully hereafter. Let us now turn to the history of this word.

In Gen. 4: 1, we find, at the birth of Cain, this declaration of Eve, as it stands in our translation: "I have gotten a man from the Lord!" The preposition "from" is not in the original. Literally it reads: "I have gotten a man, even YAHVEH!" To render the designating and emphatic particle "ETH," as it stands in this verse, by the preposition "from," or "by the aid of," is a construction well known by scholars to be—in the face of the different use of this same particle throughout the first four chapters of Genesis, including the very verse in question, where the particle "ETH" stands before every proper name made the special object of the verb; for we have "ETH" Eve, "ETH" Cain ("ETH YAHVEH"), and in the next verse again, "ETH" Abel—counter to the law of its use before proper names throughout the chronological list in the fifth chapter; in one word, at variance with every principle of Hebrew usage applicable to the case,—a construction standing amid the eight thousand one hundred and thirty enumerated instances of the particle "ETH," in its circumstances, substantially alone.

To cite in support of the exclamation of Eve as it stands in our Bible, the controverted case in Gen. 5: 24,—"Enoch walked with God,"—is not in point. The verb here, as elsewhere in parallel instances, governs its object directly and actively, requiring no preposition; this very case being often urged as a remarkable instance of the designating and defining power of the emphatic particle in question. But this would not be an instance in point, even if it were uncontroverted, it being a case of government, while Gen. 4: 1 is one of *apposition.* A citation on which such opposite views are entertained, can hardly be considered as establishing an idiom, otherwise foreign to the usage of the age in question, and entirely anomalous in the life of Eve.

A recourse to Jeremiah to determine a grammatical question of usage in Genesis, may do for a Neologist under pressure, but is rather too long a stride for a sober critic. Had Eve said, "I have gotten a man, ETH Cain,—even Cain," no deviation from the proper construction of "ETH" would have been dreamed of.

That this rendering of "ETH" is ungrammatical, has long been known. It will hereafter appear that to put YAHVEH in the mouth of Eve, as *the name of God*, is also *unhistorical*, and counter to a direct statement of the narrative. We have, then, an entirely anomalous rendering, devised to meet a difficulty existing in the minds of translators, who, ignorant of the origin and meaning of the term YAHVEH, could not understand the exclamation of Eve.

It is a conceded fact, that in the time of our translators, the Hebrew was not so well understood as now; and in cases of difficulty, much more respect was paid by them to the Greek and Latin versions of the Old Testament, that is, to the Septuagint and the Vulgate, than they deserved, or now receive.

The Septuagint, in particular, was translated some two hundred and fifty years before Christ, by a variety of authors, of very different ability, and with very different degrees of faithfulness to the original, at the command, as tradition has it, of one of the Ptolemies, a king of Egypt. Of the true origin of this version, however, nothing is really known. The Vulgate is of still later date, and of course much influenced by its predecessor.

The Septuagint translators, beside their incompetence in the Hebrew,—it having in their time become a *dead* language,—were under the influence of Jewish traditions, and also of a school of philosophers who flourished in Alexandria at that period, and whose special work appears to have been, to mystify the intellect of the civilized world, by mixing up Jewish and Oriental speculations with Platonic philosophy.

This Septuagint version was the principal assistant of our translators in their work, and its constructions were relied upon by them, in many cases, where, from want of critical knowledge, the original appeared dark or doubtful.

Now the Septuagint, on metaphysical grounds of its own, chose to use, in translating the verse to which we have alluded (Gen. 4: 1), as an equivalent for the particle "ETH," a preposition meaning "through," or "by the aid of;" — and our translators, being theologians as well as critics, following the example of their Greek predecessors, also abandon the Hebrew, and insert "from" before the term YAHVEH, or "Jehovah."

Luther, on the contrary, in his first and quaint edition of the Pentateuch and New Testament, reads: "den Man des Herrn" (the man of the

Lord, or the Lord's man); and explains this in the margin, by saying: "Whom Eve thought was the very same seed the Lord had declared would crush the serpent's head,"—in later editions substituting the more emphatic phrase, "den Man, den Herrn" (the man, the Lord); or, to follow the Hebrew more exactly, "A man, even Yahveh, or Jehovah."

We have seen what means of information the Christian world has hitherto possessed on this great subject. A set of facts, compounded of Alexandrian metaphysics and Jewish superstition, perpetuated to the English mind by a false translation of the name itself; and, as if this were not enough, by the suppression of the very name, "Jehovah," and the substitution of the unmeaning Greek term, "Kurios" (Lord, Master). What wonder that such information seems incomplete, unsatisfactory, and unmeaning!

Who is prepared to find that this memorial name, instead of being the announcement of a God "afar off," is the announcement of Christ Himself, the Deliverer of the Old, as He is the

REDEEMER of the New Testament? That the name JEHOVAH is a proclamation, a promise, and a prophecy of CHRIST, throughout all time?

Yet such is the truth which compels our convictions. It will be seen that the name "Jehovah," or YAHVEH, represented the expectation of the world; that this expectation began in the promise made to Eve, and received a *name*,—YAHVEH, HE WHO WILL BE; that this name was applied by Eve to her first-born,—transferred to God,—invoked by the Patriarchs,—affirmed to Moses,—proclaimed by the Prophets,—complete in CHRIST.

## CHAPTER II.

### BEGUN IN THE PROMISE.

THE expectation of a *Deliverer*, to which the records of every ancient people bear abundant testimony, finds its source in the First Great Promise or Prediction, that the Seed of the woman should bruise the Serpent's head: "HE shall crush thy head, and *thou* shalt wound His heel."

It was natural that Eve should expect to witness, in her *lifetime*, the realization of this prophecy. Filled with this expectation, it was natural that, looking upon her first-born, she should exclaim: "I have received *Him*, even YAHVEH!"—"even HE WHO WILL BE!"—and that she should have believed him the promised DELIVERER. That she did so believe, the record, literally interpreted, leaves no room to doubt.

It is a well-known fact in the history of language, that all primary words have originally what may be called a "pictorial" sense; that is, they express facts as made evident to the *eye*, rather than to *reason*.

Now, language *grows*, by a refining and discriminating process; namely, by the multiplication of terms, to express differences in ideas at first represented by the same term. Primary words, through some related idea, part off secondary words, and these secondaries again give out their correlatives; and thus, as language advances, it becomes more and more *abstract*, each new word expressing less in itself, and containing less of the original physical element. Thus, words representing things made evident to the *senses*, expressions having power to call up *definite images* in the mind, become gradually less and less prominent.

And so, in one respect, language loses power in its progress; for this "pictorial" element, called by the Germans "sensuous, or *sense* representation," — this inherent imagery of words, — is the element of life and beauty in style, and the very soul of poetry and narrative.

Going back, then, in this ancient history, to the childhood of the race, we find facts and events, in a certain sense, recorded as *pictures*. *Names*, also, were in those early times expressions of facts, and records of events, often of whole *histories*, capable of being drawn out in a pictorial series. It happens therefore frequently, that our refined and abstract language is incapable of giving the full "pictorial" sense of these primeval patriarchs of words.

Thus our verb "to be," purified by a long course of abstraction and theorizing, from all the "dross," as philosophy would call it, but really "life," of its original "*sense idea*," expresses no more to us than the abstract notion of existence, or than the mere logical connective in a proposition.

It is on this account entirely inadequate as a translation of the old Hebrew verb HAVAH, and its later form HAYAH, "to be," which meant primarily, rather the old English "to become;" that is, "to come about," "to begin to be or appear" (either in time or space),—as in Genesis 1:3: "Let light *be!*" that is, "spring forth," "appear." It is used, also, in the sense of "to come,"—as, Genesis 17:16: "Kings of nations shall be (or *come*) of her."

The exclamation of Eve at the birth of Cain may be expressed with more faithfulness to the original, therefore, by the rendering: "I have received Him, even—HE WHO IS TO COME!"

It can be shown, also, that this ancient root-form, HAVAH, from which comes YAHVEH, gave rise, through the idea of "breathing," its original "*sense idea*," to the two Hebrew verbs, "to be" and "to desire." From "to breathe," as the sign of existence, was derived "to be;" and from "to breathe, or pant *after*," came "to long for," "to desire."

How doubly significant, in this view, if it may be allowed a bearing, is the exclamation of Eve: "I have received Him, even—He who will be! The Promised One! The Longed For!"

We have seen that the construction given by the Septuagint, and by our translators, to

"ETH," in the exclamation of Eve,—"I have received a man," ETH YAHVEH,—departs from the original, and from all ordinary rules of grammatical interpretation bearing upon the case.

It is also, as we have already stated, not merely ungrammatical, but unhistorical, and counter to the face of the narrative; for we read, in verse 25th of this same chapter, that men did not begin to call upon the name of YAHVEH, or "Jehovah," — literally, "invoke with the name YAHVEH,"—until the birth of Enos, the grandson of Eve; and we know, further, that Eve herself uniformly spoke of God as "*Elohim*," and not YAHVEH, or "Jehovah," as appears in her conversation with the Tempter: "Elohim hath said," &c.; and in her reasons for naming Seth: "For *Elohim* hath given," &c.,—*God* standing in our translation for "Elohim," and "Lord" for YAHVEH, or "Jehovah." This use by our first parents of "*Elohim*," and not YAHVEH, or "Jehovah," as the name of God, is a point of the highest moment in its bearing upon the doctrine of the

"Fragmentary Origin of the Pentateuch," of which so much has been made in some quarters, and which will be considered hereafter.

It is not written that, upon the birth of her second son, Eve exclaimed: "I have received YAHVEH!"—HE WHO WILL BE!—on the contrary, she called him Abel, a name taken from HAVAL, "to breathe out," "to exhale," signifying, thus, in its original "*sense idea*," "that which comes to nought;" hence the name Abel, "vanity," "emptiness," "disappointment."

This name has puzzled commentators, who have suggested, by way of explanation, a prophetic foresight on the part of Eve, of the brief period and tragic termination of her son's life. But this, to say the least, is no more probable than the only other solution of the difficulty, that he received his name after death.

The latter supposition, indeed, is excluded by the narrative itself, which assumes that he was called Abel while living.

We can dispense, however, with the miracle and with the forced construction, by considering a little the circumstances of our First Parents.

They had experienced the first great disappointment. Cain was not the DELIVERER.

In view, therefore, of the probability that he would develop characteristics similar to those of their first-born, it was natural they should resolve to place no expectations, no "vain hopes," upon their second child, and that, under the influence of this feeling, they should call him *Abel*, "vanity,"—a name which, seen in this light, infolds in itself the whole history of Eve's bitter disappointment in Cain, and of the wavering of her faith in respect to the immediate appearance of the promised DELIVERER.

But, before going further, it becomes a matter of the gravest importance, to inquire what we believe, with respect to these records. The question here arises, Are these to be received as stating *historic facts?* Or, Are they to be placed upon the same footing as the Vedas of the Hindoos, and other myths of antiquity?

A strong tendency to adopt the latter view, under the guidance of a scholarship falsely so called, is creeping into the community. We deprecate such a scholarship; for it is one of words only, but blind to the point of view, impenetrable to the spirit, and jealous of the name of "*sacred*" writers.

On this basis has arisen a class of superficial authors, who, in utter ignorance of the original documents, in many cases, parade at second hand, before the world, as *facts*, theories which have long ago been retracted by their very inventors, because exploded, in the advance of true scholarship; the very schools which first thrust them forward, casting them out to perish.

Now, the mass of the community, having no means of informing themselves in regard to the latest discoveries of scholars, read eagerly every new book issued from the press, without ever raising a question on its merits as an original authority, and ignorantly suppose that, in so doing, they are keeping up with the age.

An indefiniteness of opinion, therefore, rather than a positive unbelief, with respect to the historical facts of the "Old Testament," has thus, in these days, obtained great prevalence.

It has come to pass that men are afraid to acknowledge a belief in Adam, lest, peradventure, he be an exploded myth; and are doubtful about Moses and the prophets, in the fear of an imaginary learning which may smile at their credulity.

To such it may be said, however, that, upon these points, as well as upon all others, there is no *monopoly* of learning. The case is open to every one who is willing to take time for investigation. The authorities are all on record, and the materials for judging can easily be put before the mind so that even persons of ordinary education may be placed, with regard to facts having any important relation to the conclusion, upon a footing with the most learned.

There are but two ways of looking at these early records.

One: That they are myths, or traditional stories, growing up gradually among the Hebrews, having a partly real, and partly imaginary foundation; which traditions were reduced to writing, at quite a late period, by some person or persons unknown, by way of an introduction to a general history of that people, and in order to account for the origin of their religious faith and worship.

The other: That they are statements of historic facts, described in natural language; the facts themselves being as much a part of veritable history as any, even the latest, records of the nation.

Now, the theory of myths is principally held by a class of scholars who learnedly investigate Pagan Antiquities. Finding everywhere, mixed up with absurd fables, traces of the account given us in the first chapters of Genesis, they come to the history of the Hebrew people with a preconceived idea of the mythic origin of all religions; and, instead of philosophically seeking in these first documents of the Race some literal facts or truths to account for the widely-diffused traditions, they reject the whole, as alike unworthy of credence.

But this treatment of these records cannot stand. It is inconsistent, unphilosophical, and unscholarlike. It defies all ordinary laws of criticism, trampling under foot alike rules of interpretation and principles of common sense, and rests solely upon its own self-asserted authority.

The second view would be acknowledged by the vast majority of Christendom, if pressed to a decision.

These strange and simple stories are so wonderfully related to, and interwoven with, the living facts of Christianity which we see about us,—they bear so upon their very face the stamp of the antiquity they claim, and present, apart from all considerations of religious faith, so philosophical a mode of accounting for the phenomena of the Jewish and Christian systems, and for the facts of man's consciousness,—that it is no less the dictate of reason than of common sense to acknowledge these records as *the germ* of a progressively unfolding revelation, for the completion of which we are still waiting.

These great historic phenomena, the Jewish and Christian systems, must be in some way accounted for. They originated at *some* time. When? They have been systematized and perpetuated in *some* manner. How? They tend, with all the pressure of a natural law, in one direction. Whither?

Now, if the friends of myths, or foes of Christianity, can give us a more harmonious, philosophical, or, in any respect, "less absurd" theory, of the way in which things have come to be what they are, all reasonable minds will accept the substitute. What would they propose?

Let us look at the facts.

The book of Genesis opens with a simple narrative of the creation of the world.

This great event is portrayed as a progressive picture, proceeding by successive steps, and presented under the divisions of a week of time.

The fact and its presentation need no discussion here. Science reads in her "rocky folios" an order of creation proceeding by successive stages, and affirms this order to be the parallel of the Divine picture.

Who will deny her teachings, coming in the words and with the authority of one whose name, honored in two hemispheres, stands first in the department he has so beautifully systematized and presented? *

It is a truth of *science* that the plateau of Central Asia, described in Genesis as the birthplace of man, was the portion of the earth's surface first prepared for such a resident.

This fact, as well as the yet broader one, that language and history, traced back to their primary sources, converge toward that spot, are truths utterly independent of Revelation, and from which no one acquainted with the latest results of scientific research will dissent.

Taking up, then, the narrative at the creation of man.

Is it absurd to suppose:

That man was formed from dust?

That he was originally made innocent and pure?

That such a being was placed in a garden, or Paradise?

To the first inquiry, surely the great procession daily returning to dust is a solemn and

* Prof. James D. Dana, New Haven.

perpetual response. The two latter need no argument. Probably no one could be found who would venture to assert that the present condition of man fulfills the original design of his creation.

The "tree of life," also, is susceptible of a most natural explanation.

To man in Paradise it was as the ark in the wilderness to the wandering Israelites, or the temple of Solomon to the Jewish nation,—the sign and symbol of God's presence, and of that communion with Him by which man is a partaker in eternal life. A simple, natural object, but living and growing, was thus selected and set apart as a temple of God in the garden,—fit representative of the perennial life and growth of a sinless and immortal soul.

The fruit of the "tree of life," of which man was suffered to partake, and to which he had a right, by virtue of his *innocence*, was forfeited when he became disobedient; and, lest he should still presume upon his continued right to that symbol of eternal life, he was exiled from the garden.

That this is the explanation of the "tree of life," seems clear from the fact that in Revelation, under a figure borrowed from the first Paradise, the redeemed of the second Paradise are spoken of as having a *right* to the "tree of life,"—a *right* of which they are made partakers through Christ.

Christ also speaks of Himself as the "bread of life," and says: "If any man eat of this 'bread' he shall live forever." In a precisely corresponding sense, the fruit of the "tree of life" may have symbolized to Adam in Paradise a Divine communion.

With regard to the temptation, and its attendant circumstances. Do we not know that evil is in the world? Why should we, then, believe that the great adversary who assailed in vain the second Adam is a myth in his triumph over the first?

There are many minds to whom their instinctive recoil from the serpent tribe testifies to something more than the natural fear of physical evil. This hatred of the serpent is a feeling so widely diffused, that it may be said to be common to the race, and fulfills in itself a part of the curse: "I will put enmity between thy seed and her seed." This fact, so far as it may be allowed weight, is on the side of the truth of the narrative.

Let us look now at a point of profound historic interest, but one which has been more thoroughly misconceived than perhaps any other in this narrative. We refer to the "cherubic symbols." The account of their inauguration reads thus: "So he drove out the man; and he placed at the east of the garden of Eden cherubim, and a flaming sword, which turned every way, to keep the way of the tree of life."

Probably if our translators had used the expression, "to *preserve* the way of the tree of life," instead of "to *keep*" the same, the prevalent idea of the design of God in instituting these symbols would have been totally different. Yet this is the meaning of the original; in which, also, the "*way* of the tree of life," rather than the *tree itself*, is made emphatic. How different a conception is this from that of our primers and catechisms, in which an angel is made to brandish a flaming sword at Adam, for the purpose of keeping him out of the garden. Now neither angel nor sword appear in the original.

Two mysterious, supernatural, winged figures, and between them a sword-like, revolving flame, were stationed eastward from Eden, not so much to keep Adam *out* of the garden, as to preserve the knowlege of the "way of the tree of life" *in* the world. A glance at the original at once shows this to be the meaning. To man in his altered relations "the cherubim," with the flaming fire between them, took the place of the "tree of life" in the world, by a direct appeal to the *eye*, telling of judgment, and yet, under the relations of the promise, speaking of mercy.

These were the symbols of Divinity, perpetually present to man before the flood, but "every imagination of the thoughts of his heart was only evil continually," "and all flesh had corrupted his way upon the earth," "and the earth, was filled with violence." Yet *idolatry* did not and could not arise among those who looked upon these flaming symbols of a present God. The flood came, and swept away the symbols; the traditions were carried over, and appear in the idolatries of the succeeding ages.

The cherubim are found again in connection with the ark made by Moses in the wilderness. They are represented as shadowing and looking towards the mercy-seat. They appear also in the same manner in Solomon's Temple; they are not definitely described, but the impression conveyed is like that of the first cherubim,—supernatural, winged figures, neither human nor angelic, but combining the idea of both. An image was thus presented to the mind, of an exalted order of beings continually rendering worship to their God, who was also the Creator of man; a representation designed to exalt and purify the worship of man, and which he, in his proneness to degrade the idea of God to his own level, could hardly do without.

Another extraordinary mention of figures, sometimes incorrectly called by this name, is made by Ezekiel. Had it not been for the modern discovery of the great historic fossils of Nineveh, the world would have remained without light upon this most interesting subject. It appears, however, that a part of the scenery of his wondrous vision was taken from the very walls about the prophet, — literal transcripts from the symbolic imagery of Assyria, in which we discern the original divinely-instituted cherubim corrupted into the insignia of idolatry.

In the vision on the banks of the Chebar, these figures of Assyrian type support the pavement of the throne of Jehovah, who sits above them in unspeakable glory. They move parallel with the wheels of His providence. At His bidding they go forward. At His bidding they stand still. A more impressive representation of the supremacy of Jehovah over the wisdom of the Chaldeans, the oppressors of His people, could not be conceived.

That the original symbols of Divinity should have been corrupted by a portion of the human family, is not surprising, and it is certainly most interesting to observe and identify even in idolatrous forms, those winged sentinels of the "way of life" who kept their station in the antediluvian world.

To deduce "the cherubim" of the Temple, of the Ark, and of Eden, those purely supernatural forms, from the idolatrous figures of Nineveh, is unphilosophical.

To deduce the Assyrian figures from the Cherubic symbols, has, to say the least, the advantage of probability on its side.

The Assyrian figures must have grown out of some traditions — what more likely than those of the world before the flood? — especially when in this light, almost every one of their sacred symbols is at once explained. In the winged figures we behold the ancient "cherubim"—in the "sacred fire," "the revolving flame"—in the "sacred tree," the "tree of life." We find *historically*, exactly what we should expect to find on the assumption of the literal truth of these records—that the nations nearest the original centre, preserved in their sacred symbols the traditions of the facts of this narrative.

May we not discern also, in this view, a most natural explanation of the fire-worship of the ancient Persians?

Surely a fire which flamed for two thousand years, as a symbol of Divinity, could hardly have failed to leave traces in the world's history.

How reasonable to suppose that these symbols would be reproduced after the flood. Man, feeling the need of worship, naturally looks back for some tradition of the beginning of all things, upon which to found his worship. Accordingly, among those ancient races appearing first in History upon the flanks of the Great Central Plateau, is seen the purest form of these traditions in the symbolic "sacred fire;" and among the Assyrians, the worship of this "sacred fire," with the addition of the "sacred tree," and "winged creatures" of divers shapes, answering to the ancient "cherubim."

But whatever may be conceded to these inductions, one point at least of great interest, which has hitherto baffled Oriental scholars, is now clearly set at rest. The ASHERAH, or "sacred grove" of the idolatrous Jews, was the "sacred tree" of the Assyrians.

The "record chamber" of Kouyunjik, when its tablets shall have been deciphered, may give us facts outrunning our conjectures.

The History of these ancient nations is fast becoming, in respect of certainty, like one of the natural sciences. Entombed memorials of the ages, brought to light day by day, are putting to silence the wisdom of the wisest philosophers of History. Safety lies now, only in reasoning from the *known* to the unknown. The line of induction on these subjects, must run parallel with the discoveries of modern investigators, and having put together all the facts to be commanded, further results must be waited for.

But to return to the History of our first parents.

It is impossible to give a just interpretation to these ancient records without duly considering also the Theology of the period.

In that age, which may be called the "Age of Paradise," the first step was taken, in the science of Revealed Theology. The *promise* was given, and this promise was the word of God to the Race of Adam.

It was their only material for Theological discussion, and contained the *all*, for which they could hope. Before them was the creeping serpent, the symbol of the evil to be overcome, the actual and present representative of one side of the great contest predicted between the Deceiver of Eve, and the promised Deliverer. The *Evil* was in the world, but *where* was the Good? When would *He*, the Representative of the other side of the great contest, make His appearance? How natural to suppose He would come at *once*. What a theme of expectation then, would be this Coming One — this promised DELIVERER.

We have noticed the exultation of Eve at the birth of Cain, evinced by her exclamation: "I have received Him, even the Coming One!"

We may derive from this record of the expectation of Eve, that Cain was to be the Deliverer, a reason why the first-born of the Race of Adam should have been allowed to become a representative of violence and wrong, of the possible wickedness of a human being.

It served to show the true nature and results of sin, and to lead men away from the hope of a merely human Deliverer.

Had the characteristics of the first child been those of Abel, the Theology of the Promise might have remained longer in doubt.

We have seen that the term YAHVEH, or "Jehovah," was used by Eve, to represent the promise and the expectation of a DELIVERER, and was applied to her first-born.

It was transferred to God.

## CHAPTER III.

### TRANSFERRED TO GOD.

PROCEEDING with the narrative, we have, in connection with the birth of Enos, the record to which we have already alluded.

"Then began men to call upon the name of YAHVEH," or "Jehovah." Literally: "Then was begun invocation with the name YAHVEH."

That this has reference merely to the worship of God, cannot be; for we know that Abel worshipped, and that Seth was in the line of the faithful.

Why then this reference to the first invocation of YAHVEH?

The writer has given in the form of a genealogical table, a record of nearly two thousand years, with here and there only an isolated way-mark in the shape of a fact.

We simply find, therefore, a brief statement, that at some time in the interval, this name, with its Promise and its Hope, was transferred to God. Apart from this statement however, does not the fact that Cain was called YAHVEH, and supposed to be the DELIVERER, and afterwards that God was invoked as YAHVEH, show that men had transferred their hope of a Deliverer, from man, to God Himself?

Does not the fact also, that this transfer was recorded at all, show it to be a point of great Historical interest?

The distinction throughout the Pentateuch in the use of "Elohim" and "Jehovah," or "God" and "Lord," as these names are rendered in our Translation, is observable by even a casual reader: "Elohim" appearing to have been an older name than "Jehovah," and the history showing a gradual change from the use of "Elohim" as the name of God to that of "Jehovah" or YAHVEH.

Throughout Genesis these distinctions are quite apparent, the two names seeming for awhile to run parallel; "Jehovah" gradually superseding "Elohim," until in Exodus it is solemnly adopted by God Himself and proclaimed as His "memorial" name to all generations, after which time it is used almost exclusively, "Elohim" appearing only occasionally. This distinction in the use of these names, has been seized upon by the enemies of Revelation as a point of attack.

They have undertaken the most deadly and thorough assault upon the antiquity of the Pentateuch and the chronicles therein contained, that the world has seen. Yet, what have they accomplished?

They have developed the alarming circumstance, that historical records actually preceded Moses; — that the great Legislator had documents before him older than the exodus from Egypt; — that, possibly, Genealogical Lists were accompanied by scattered yet decisive mention of well-known Historical facts; — and yet more, that these Lists might have been used, and these facts employed by Moses, often in the very language of their first record.

This great discovery has been dignified as the "Fragmentary Origin of the Pentateuch."

Whatever is originally fragmentary, is in the opinion of these critics, of course, fabulous. Therefore, Creation is a myth — the Flood a tradition — Moses himself is quietly extinguished in the "Mosaic Writer" — the Pentateuch passes forward into that comfortable solvent of all Historical difficulties, "the times of the Judges" — and thus we have the "Origin and Progress of the Mosaic Mythology," and the "Later Literary Treatment of these Legends." — (De Wette.)

Truly, they who will not hear Moses and the Prophets will not be persuaded though one rose from the dead! Granting the prior records which might have been inferred as probable, even could they not be critically discriminated, why should they not have been employed by Moses in accordance with the will of Him, who talked with the Historian as a man talketh face to face with his friend?

But will it be credited, that this whole scheme of "Mosaic Mythology" begins with, and turns upon the assumption that "*Jehovah*" is a *modern name?* That the presence of this venerable term — hoar with the frost of ages — old with an antiquity lost from the language ere the Pentateuch was penned — standing out the equivalent of the exclamation of the first mother in the joy of her new-born child — that this venerable term is the evidence and proof of a "modern writer" — of a "Mosaic Mythology" — of a later "literary Legend!" Yet such is their dependence. But Truth shall be established even in the mouth of the King's enemies. These are the *very men*, who, for an end they meant not, have put on record the analysis and derivation of this very term. They could not see its *History*, for they would not read its meaning.

Now the true History of the name "Jehovah" is the key to the interpretation of these records.

But before proceeding to show this, we will consider a question which may be asked here:

What are the evidences of prior records?

Let the reader change, in Gen. 6: 5, "God" to "Lord," in which sole instance in these first documents our Translators have departed from their rule of translation with respect to these names.

He will then see that the book of Genesis is made up, in several instances, of duplicate accounts of the various events which it records, together with Genealogical Lists of the different families of those early times. He will see also that some of these Lists and accounts use "Elohim" or "God," and others "Jehovah" or "Lord," as the name of God, and have often the appearance of being contemporaneous with the events recorded. This use of antecedent records is much more manifest in the original than in the translation, and is traceable by various points not apparent to the English reader. These fragments have been distinguished by critics as the "Elohistic" and "Yahvistic" Documents, and out of this distinction has grown up a great scheme for the demolition of the Pentateuch, or rather of its credibility.

The advocates of this scheme however are divided among themselves, one party holding that the Pentateuch is a collection of isolated fragments, separable by the distinctive names

"Elohim" and "Jehovah," and put together by some person or persons unknown anywhere about the times of the Judges, or even later.

The other, that it contains two ancient and general accounts, distinguished as the "Elohistic" and "Yahvistic" narratives. The former, or "Elohistic," embracing a consecutive History, running through Genesis, and traceable throughout the Pentateuch; while the latter, or "Yahvistic" narrative, cannot be framed into a connected history, though dispersed in fragments through Genesis, and prevailing in the rest of the Pentateuch. The details of this view are unnecessary.

The second school pronounces the first superficial and superannuated, and in fact the first school has disappeared as an authority.

The second school also has its difficulties, the Documents being so interlocked as to be often inseparable, except by the free use of the "internal sense" of the critic in the transposition of unaccommodating passages.

It was fashionable in the time of De Wette, who represents the first school, to cry "interpolation;" when the text did not suit this "internal sense!"

The critics of the present day, charging all want of harmony between their theories and the text to "transposition," and the "tendency of the writer," quietly ridicule the uncritical methods of their predecessors "the Fragmentists." Both schools however in respect to the writer of the Pentateuch might appropriately use the language of the Israelites: "As for this *Moses*, we wot not what is become of him."

Following the lead of Niebuhr, who decomposed the history of the Kings of Rome into ancient ballads, and of Wolfe, who dissected Homer into fragmentary odes, these Theorists apply the same method of conjecture to the Pentateuch, and making no allowance whatever for the manner in which these records have been preserved and perpetuated, they conclude them all alike under the head of "Myths:"—hence the title "Mosaic Mythology."

This whole scheme has been elaborated out of just the materials already presented to the reader, and no more. Any one who will attentively study these records in the light of the hints given, will be in all important respects as capable of forming a "theory of fragments" as the most learned, or most audacious of these critics.

It will be seen that the great point to be Historically accounted for, and one which these Apostles of Conjecture do not touch, is the fact that the original name of God, "Elohim," was superseded by a second name, "Jehovah." This change is in itself extraordinary, and could not have taken place except for some grand Historical reason. This reason must be sought in the narrative itself.

We have said that the History of the name "Jehovah" is the key to the interpretation of these documents. It not only explains the change from "Elohim" to "Jehovah," but accounts with perfect consistency for the alternations in the Documents themselves. A critical examination of the book of Genesis will show that "Elohim," or "God," was first in use as the name of God; "Jehovah" or Yahveh, not appearing until the time of Enos, in connection with whose birth it is recorded, "Then began men to call upon the name of YAHVEH, or 'Jehovah,'" *literally* "began to invoke with the name YAHVEH." A cursory reader of the records might be inclined to dispute this statement. It will, however, be found to bear examination. "Jehovah Elohim" or "Lord God" indeed appears in the second chapter of the narrative, but this will be seen to be the use of the name by the compiler or writer of the account,—Eve making use invariably of "Elohim" as the name of God, throughout her lifetime. It is evident that both the writers and the compiler of these fragmentary accounts had an "internal historical sense," which would not allow them to put such an anachronism in the mouth of Eve, as the use by her of "Jehovah" would have been. This same use of "Elohim" instead of "Jehovah" holds true in respect to the only other character of the narrative, introduced as speaking,—that is, the Tempter or Serpent. After the birth of Enos, a change is apparent, the name "Jehovah" appearing in the mouth of the next speaker, and, as has been stated, continuing to be used throughout the rest of the Pentateuch as the name of God, side by side with " Elohim," which it finally supersedes.

These facts, taken in connection with the Theology of the period, which was the " Theology of the Promise," are in themselves a statement of the Historical growth and use of this name. It first represented the promised Deliverer.

The Deliverer was expected immediately to appear.

Cain was supposed to be, and was called Yahveh, The Deliverer.

The hope of a human Deliverer was given up.

God was invoked as Yahveh, The Deliverer.

How the name came to be directly transferred to God, is not recorded. That He sanctioned the transfer is evident; for when God declared Himself to Moses under the name Yahveh, or " Jehovah," He does not proclaim it as altogether new, but rather, as will be shown hereafter, reaffirms it as an old Historical name which had lost its former significance.

This much is certain, however, that the name grew out of the expectation of a DELIVERER, and was transferred to God, who at the birth of Enos began to be invoked as YAHVEH, or "Jehovah."

Let us apply the ascertained facts to the further elucidation of these records.

We have stated, that "Elohim" was the only name of God in use, until the birth of Enos. After that time we find "Elohim," the old name, still continues, the new name "Jehovah" appearing, however, in the mouths of the speakers, and also in duplicate accounts of the two Elohistic narratives, "The Creation," and "The Deluge." The "Yahvistic" account of the Creation, originating necessarily after the time of Enos, and for the purpose, probably, of identifying "YAHVEH," or "Jehovah" the "Deliverer," with "Elohim the Creator;" the two sets of Historical fragments throughout Genesis, bearing the marks of having been *written together*, or formed into a connected narrative by a later writer, who uses "YAHVEH" as the name of God current in his times. This writer is generally supposed to be *Moses*, and since there is not a shadow of authority either internal or external, for setting him aside, as the author or compiler of the book of Genesis, the general belief upon this point is not only reasonable, but in accordance with the laws of criticism.

This simple explanation, drawn from the records themselves, will be found to solve the exceedingly complicated problem of "Elohistic" and "Yahvistic Documents," so bewildering to modern critics.

The assumption that the book of Genesis contains historical fragments, many of them contemporaneous, or nearly so, with the events they record, may be thought without sufficient foundation. It is hardly to be supposed however that the great events prior to the Flood, and immediately after, would remain unrecorded till the time of Moses. It is certain that Genealogical tables were in some way preserved, and by whatever method they were handed down, orally, pictorially, ideographically or otherwise, the incidents and events, appearing in connection with them, must have originated at the same time, and have been perpetuated in like manner.

We have said that these Records bear upon their face the stamp of the antiquity they claim. Their fragmentary appearance itself is a strong evidence of antiquity.

The curt, disconnected paragraphs speak for themselves of a time when the art of writing or recording did not admit of prolixity; the earliest stages of that art being marked by short and succinct statements of facts.

The character of the fragments also is that of the highest antiquity, and not at all like anything "got up" at a later period. We will cite as an instance, a waif of antediluvian song, which has come down to us in the form of Hebrew poetry or parallelism. It is interesting as being the first poetry on record, as well as serving to illustrate the character of the descendants of Cain, who appear to have inherited the disposition of their ancestor, and who probably did much towards filling the earth with violence.

This fragment occurs in the fourth chapter of Genesis; and appears to be a song of triumph, over a fallen adversary, sung by Lamech, in the presence of his wives:

"Adah and Zillah,
Hear my voice;
Wives of Lamech,
Listen to my words:

"For a man have I slain,
For wounding me;
Yea, a young man
For smiting me.

"If sevenfold
Cain be avenged;
Yea, Lamech,
Seventy and seven."

It will be noticed that this song occurs in connection with the first mention of musical instruments, and that it is transmitted to us as a memento of a musical family,—Jubal, the son of Lamech, being specified as "the father of all such as handle the harp and organ." This is doubtless a Hebrew edition of one of the ballads set to music by Jubal himself. It is impossible to convey, in another language, the rhythmic beat, and dancing movement of the original, so apparent as to suggest at once the idea of motion to music.

This primeval ballad, and the memorials of those ancient times with which it is interlocked, gray with an antiquity that laughs at a Veda or an Avesta as modern, are the heritage of the race,—they belong not to the Hebrews, but to our common humanity,—and constitute the proper background of all History.

The manner in which these Documents have been perpetuated, finds no analogy in the Myths of Rome, or the Odes of Homer. To ignore the historical grounds of difference in their respective cases, is to set aside all integrity of criticism.

The same remark holds true in comparing these with the traditions of the Creation and the origin of the Race, existing in other languages.

All such traditions are full of inherent impossibilities, with no pretence to a consecutive account, and incapable of being framed into a connected or consistent History. They are acknowledged myths. Whoever would study them, must take the attitude of a seeker for gleams of truth, amid mazes of gross absurdities and contradictions, and if by chance he discover what he seeks, it is like finding gems in a heap of rubbish.

This statement cannot be denied by even the most devoted admirer of myths.

The accounts of Genesis on the other hand are inherently probable, consecutive, and consistent. They contain moreover in themselves a most reasonable ground of credibility.

Every scholar is aware of the scrupulous vigilance with which the purity of the Hebrew text of the Old Testament was guarded among the Jews. The question of the integrity of these first records is thus a question outside of the history of the Hebrews as a nation. If there are myths in Genesis they must have originated before the time of Moses.

Now the genealogies themselves show that Shem the ancestor, and for one hundred and fifty years the cotemporary of Abraham, was himself cotemporary with men, one of whom lived two centuries with Adam. Abraham therefore had access to the "very best authorities" with respect to the events prior to his time.

We know that Abraham was the founder of that Divinely superintended Jewish nation, through whom these records of common interest to the race have been preserved and transmitted to us. That these also were Divinely superintended, who can doubt?

In them is laid the corner-stone of the Church—the Promise of Redemption.

In them is found the first Gospel—the Gospel of the Promise.

They make mention of the first preachers of righteousness,—Enoch and Noah,—and they contain the transfer to God of the name which gives unity to the Church throughout all time,—the name Yahveh, Deliverer.

## CHAPTER IV.

### INVOKED BY THE PATRIARCHS.

The first act of Noah on leaving the ark, was to build an altar to Yahveh, or "Jehovah."

That this name of God, had, prior to the Flood, in a great measure superseded the original name "Elohim," is evident from its use in the narrative. It is natural however to suppose, that the idea originally associated with the name Yahveh, would be but vaguely retained by the immediate descendants of Noah, and by the Patriarchs. The fact of deliverance from the Flood which had buried the earth beneath its waves, would indeed be associated, in the mind of Noah, with gratitude to God as Deliverer, and to this Deliverer he would offer the sacrifice of thanksgiving. But the hope of a restoration to an earthly Paradise must have departed, in the great change which blotted from the face of the earth all traces of its former existence. Thus while the church of the antediluvian world had, under the Theology of the Promise, fixed its hopes upon a Deliverer who was to restore them to the original Paradise, the great image filling the minds of Noah and his immediate descendants, must have been that of the Ark, bearing over to a renovated earth a single family, saved from the common ruin. Their Theology would be that of "Past Deliverance," and the name "Jehovah" thus associated with that great fact would gradually lose its primary and prophetic meaning, and come to represent the general and special care of God over his children.

The Theology of the Promise must have been vague indeed in their minds, and the name Yahveh, or "Jehovah," though designating to them a near and peculiar relation of God to man would not so much carry the mind forward to the Hope, as backward to the *fact* of Deliverance. So "Jehovah" as the special Guardian of their Father Noah, would be the

God of his children, and of their children's children.

But with the new world was to begin a new economy. The first step was to be taken towards the preparation for the coming of YAHVEH, The Promised One. A people was to be selected and trained in a special school, the arrangements and discipline of which were appointed for a single end,—to educate them to understand and appreciate the manifestation of Divinity, to appear in the coming YAHVEH.

If the highest possible expression of the love of God was to be the offering up of His only begotten son to die, then, before the fullness of love displayed in that Divine sacrifice could be comprehended by Humanity, it must itself be trained through a system of sacrifices to a familiarity with the idea.

Thus, the Sacrifice,—that wonderful symbol of Divine Love, of a love which gives itself up, even to the blood, which is "the life,"—was instituted at the very gate of Eden, and appears on every page of succeeding History.

But the Theology of the Promise was to be

reinstituted under a more *specific* relation to humanity.

The promise made to Eve in the form of a general prophetic statement relating to the race, and altogether indefinite as to the time of its fulfillment, was to be rendered more definite in time, and more particular in respect to the tribe or nation in which YAHVEH was to appear.

Accordingly, Abram was selected as the founder of a chosen people under the Promise: "I will make of thee a great nation, and in thee shall all families of the earth be blessed;" and so is taken the first great step towards the development of the original promise. The history of this development is a progress from the first general prophecy, to more and more specific statements concerning YAHVEH, and His work. The promise to Abram directed the vague and universal expectation of the world to the particular nation of which he was to be the founder; and the time of the coming of YAHVEH was rendered more definite by the implication that a great nation must first arise, and possess the land of Canaan, before the promised blessing would appear.

These special promises to Abraham that he, yet childless, should become the Father of a people, mighty, and numerous, destined to possess the land in which he himself was a sojourner and stranger, must have filled his mind with wonder and expectation, and the knowledge that God was able to perform that which He had promised, must have been the stronghold of his faith.

*El Shaddai*, God Almighty, would therefore be the name of God upon which he would dwell with peculiar confidence and trust.

As *El Shaddai*, therefore, God confirms his covenant with Abraham, and as *El Shaddai*, gives to Jacob the name of "Israel,"—renewing the promise made to Abraham, in a still more specific manner,—assuring "Israel," that *he*, out of all the descendants of Abraham, should become the Father of the chosen people. Thus the name *El Shaddai* would represent to Abraham and his successors in the line of the chosen, a Mighty Promiser of blessings, and would be comprehended by them, in a way in which YAHVEH, or "Jehovah," could not be, although the latter was still in use as the old historic name of the God of their Fathers, and as representing promises "afar off." Thus the same God appeared at different times under different names, and according as one name bore a more immediate relation to the circumstances in which it was affirmed, it overshadowed in significance the others.

In this view may be found the explanation of an apparent contradiction in the narrative in respect to the use of the name YAHVEH, or "Jehovah," by the Patriarchs; we find it upon every page of their history, and yet, on turning to Ex. 6: 3, it is there stated by God Himself, that by His name YAHVEH, He was not known to them.

This apparent inconsistency has been a stumbling-block to many, and has even been seized upon by some, who lay claim to superior scholarship, as an objection to the credibility of these records.

The first rudiments of a knowledge of any foreign tongue, however, ought to be sufficient to suggest the explanation of this entirely superficial difficulty.

In translating from one language into another, *everything* of course depends upon accuracy in the words chosen to represent the sense of the original.

Thus, in almost any foreign language, a verb having the sense of "to comprehend," "to understand," may often be translated by the English verb "to know." In very many instances however the verb "to know" would not give the sense of the original.

The case under consideration is an instance of the folly of building an objection upon a *translation* merely. The objection disappears at once upon reference to the original. The verb there used, means "to comprehend," "to understand," and is very inaccurately and inadequately rendered by "to know." Literally it reads: "And by my name YAHVEH, was I not 'comprehended,' or 'understood' by them." It properly conveys the meaning "to see with the mind," "to understand by means of explanatory circumstances." As in the return of the Dove to the Ark with an olive-leaf, then Noah "knew" that the waters were abated;

and in the sacrifice of Manoah, when the Angel of the Lord ascended in the flame of the altar and returned not, then Manoah "knew" he was an Angel of the Lord.

An instance by which the sense of this word may be tested, occurs, in Isaiah 6: 9. "Seeing they shall see and shall not *perceive*," that is, "understand," "comprehend." The word here correctly rendered "perceive," is precisely the one, which, in the case under consideration, our Translators have given as "know."

The relative difference between "seeing" and "perceiving" corresponds exactly to that between "knowing" and "comprehending," as will appear by substituting in the above example the latter forms of expression, thus, "knowing they shall know, but shall not comprehend."

This simple explanation of an apparently direct contradiction in the narrative, may suggest a solvent for similar cases throughout the sacred records.

To a mind in any degree aware of the difficulty of rendering with perfect accuracy an expression of one language, by words taken from another, it would seem almost a miracle if such apparent inconsistencies did not sometimes occur in the course of the translation of a long narrative. When we add to this the consideration of the fact that the Hebrew was but imperfectly understood in the time of our Translators, we have elements for a vindication of cases of difficulty, which, in any particular instance, ought to be enough to hold a scholarly mind in suspense, till the case has at least been subjected to the test of reference to the original.

Thus this instance of alleged contradiction which we have considered, not only is seen to be perfectly consistent with the rest of the narrative, but becomes in itself a testimony to the significance of the name YAHVEH, or "Jehovah," in its historical relation to the race. The original prophetic meaning of this term, and its associated idea DELIVERANCE, bore no such immediate relation to the exigencies of the Patriarchs, as to make that name "comprehended" by them from the circumstances of their own experience. The expectation of a return to an Earthly Paradise having died out of the world, the more spiritual idea of "Deliverance from *sin*," could not arise to take the place of that departed hope, except through a course of training by which it should be developed in the mind of humanity.

Before the great want of a Deliverer from *sin* could be so impressed upon the world that it would be prepared for such a Deliverer, a school must be instituted, and a *nation* trained to express that want, and as Corypheus in the great chorus of Humanity, call upon YAHVEH as a DELIVERER from *Sin*.

The era of the Patriarchs thus intervenes as a kind of transition period in the history of the Church, between the idea of YAHVEH as the restorer of the original Paradise, and YAHVEH as Deliverer from sin. The one having passed away, and the other not having arisen, the theology of the First Promise was for a time apparently in a state of suspense.

And yet YAHVEH, the representative of that promise, appears everywhere in the narrative as the constant guardian and friend of the Patriarchs. He took upon Himself the form and attributes of man when He appeared to Abraham on the plains of Mamre. He ate and drank, He walked and talked with him, as a *man.* He reasoned with Abraham and allowed Himself to be persuaded, as a *man.* As a *man* He contended with Jacob, and yielded before him, yet He superintended every act and punished and rewarded as God, and as a Father, the Fathers of the Patriarchal Church. His government was precisely similar to that exercised by them over their families, and the test of their faith was that of implicit reliance upon Him, and obedience to His commands. It was thus the Patriarchal era in two senses.

Thus also YAHVEH, or "Jehovah," taking upon Himself the form of Humanity, and at the same time revealing Himself as God, brought the Fathers of the Patriarchal Church into the most intimate relationship to Himself, through the idea of "friendship," instituting by this means the closest personal intercourse between the individual soul and God.

In this way also, as a preparation for the great economy of Law, was developed in the world an ideal of individual nearness to, and communion with God,—a preparation most requisite for a Theocratic government of Law, in which the *Nation* would necessarily take precedence of the *Individual*, and the character of *Lawgiver* supersede that of *Father*, so that without this foundation "type" of individual piety, perpetually present throughout the Mosaic economy, in the character of Abraham "the friend of God," the idea of personal relationship to God could hardly have grown up in the Jewish Church.

Thus Abraham stood to that Church, as its founder and ideal type, in a relation like that of Christ in His Humanity, to the Christian Church,—its founder and ideal type.

It was fitting also that the Father of the great school of sacrifices should express, by His own act, the highest ideal of that faith which in the Mosaic Church would be counted as "righteousness," and that the sacrifice of Isaac should typify that Divine sacrifice yet to take place in the world,—the offering up of "the only begotten son."

In this way was secured to the Jewish mind a comprehension of "sacrifice," as an expression of perfect obedience, faith and love, even without a .direct knowledge of the relation of YAHVEH to the Divine Sacrifice.

And so, as introductory to the great organized expression in the Mosaic system, of the relation of "sacrifice" to "Law," was implanted in the world an *individual* expression of the relation of "sacrifice" to "Faith," and also, the Divine idea of a "self-sacrifice," willing to offer up that which is dearest, even to the "life."

We have traced the history of YAHVEH, and the unfolding promise of His Great Deliverance, from the first vague and general prophecy to Eve, to the more specific yet still undefined promise to Abraham.

At the end of the Patriarchal Era the prophetic utterances of Jacob give greater distinctness to the character and work of the coming DELIVERER.

The dying Patriarch in a series of brief but comprehensive sentences, marks out the future career of each one of his descendants, and in the course of this series utters two distinct prophecies of "the Coming One," with an ejaculation of disappointment that he has not "known" the Deliverance of YAHVEH, for which he has waited.

The first of these prophecies is in the benediction of Judah. After assigning to him the precedence over his other sons, Israel continues: "The sceptre shall not depart from Judah, nor a Lawgiver from between his feet, until SHILOH come, and unto HIM shall the gathering of 'the peoples' be."

And thus does the unfolding promise become more and more *specific*. From the "nation" is singled out a "tribe," whose preëminence, it is declared, shall be maintained until the appearing of the Great Coming One, "Shiloh," "Prince of Peace," to take the place of Judah in the World, and to whom "the gathering of the peoples" shall be.

The *character* also of the kingdom superseding and transcending that of Judah is given as "peace," implying a "spiritual" kingdom whose universality, and whose moral sway, is inferred from the expression "the gathering of the peoples," as contrasted with the coercive rule of the "sceptre" and the "Lawgiver," and as doing away with the limitations of tribe and nation.

In this single prophecy, then, we have a prediction of the great general facts of the Coming and Kingdom of YAHVEH, HE WHO WILL BE. We next have a recognition of YAHVEH, or "Jehovah," as DELIVERER.

In the benediction of Dan, Jacob makes use of a figure recalling to us the language of the first Promise.

"Dan shall be a serpent by the way, an adder in the path, that biteth the horse heels, so that his rider shall fall backward."

In immediate connection with this prophecy, and as if suggested by it, comes the remarkable and apparently isolated exclamation,—"I have waited for thy DELIVERANCE, O YAHVEH!"

What more natural than that in characterizing Dan as a "serpent" or "adder" biting at the heels of his adversaries, the thought of the Great Adversary, "The Serpent," and of the Great DELIVERER, YAHVEH, should take possession of the mind of the Patriarch, and that he should give utterance to an ejaculation of disappointment at not having "known" the DELIVERANCE he himself foretold, and for which he had all his lifetime "waited."

Lastly: In the blessing of Joseph we find a distinct intimation of the superhuman character of the Coming DELIVERER.

In speaking of the triumph of Joseph over his enemies, this triumph is attributed to the "Mighty One of Jacob," by whom he had been upheld, and from whence was to come the "Shepherd," "Stone," or "Rock" of Israel.

Thus far then the original Promise has unfolded itself:

In the assumption by God of the name of the Coming One, "YAHVEH."

The Promise to Abraham, that the Coming One should appear in the "nation" of which he was to be founder.

The Prophecies of Jacob:

That the Coming One should appear in the "tribe" of Judah.

That the Kingdom represented by Judah should give place to the Kingdom of the Coming One.

That this latter Kingdom should be a Kingdom of "Peace."

That it should be greater than the Kingdom of the "Sceptre" and "Lawgiver," gathering in "the peoples" without distinction of tribe or nation.

That the "Shepherd," the "Rock of Israel," was to be from the "Mighty One" of Jacob.

That YAHVEH or "Jehovah" was to be the Author of a Great DELIVERANCE.

Then comes a break in the history of the descendants of Jacob.

Four hundred years of bondage are passed over in silence; and as if the story were not so much of a nation or people, as of YAHVEH, THE DELIVERER, we are taken directly from the recognition by Jacob, of YAHVEH as a

Deliverer for whom he had "waited," but whom he had not "known," to a Great Fact of Deliverance, in connection with which we find this affirmation to the suffering Israelites,—Ye shall "*know*" that I am Yahveh, Deliverer.

## CHAPTER V.

### AFFIRMED TO MOSES.

THE Promise contained in the Name YAHVEH is now in a subordinate sense to be fulfilled.

He, who had been invoked in the Adamic Dispensation, as the Author of an undeveloped Hope, originating in the Promise to Eve,—by the Patriarchs, as a Mighty Promiser of blessings, more specific, yet still remote,—enters upon the work of fulfilment. He is now to become the Actual Deliverer and Theocratic Head of the Nation of Israel.

In this Deliverance also, being inaugurated that greater Deliverance to be wrought in the world, He now affirms His ancient name YAHVEH, "Jehovah," HE WHO WILL BE, and by the connection in which it is proclaimed, takes upon Himself forever, under this Memorial Name, the character of DELIVERER.

We thus come to the consideration of the great event of the Ancient world. God enters into History as the Leader of a People. He now for the first time proclaims a Name, expressive of a permanent and universal relation. He sets forth this Name with the most solemn and emphatic formality,—under three Divine affirmations,—and adopts it as His own, His great and standing Memorial from generation to generation.

What are these affirmations? They are recorded in Exodus 3: 14, in reply to the question by Moses,—What shall I say to Israel's children? And God said,—

I WILL BE WHO I WILL BE.

Here the Hebrew verb HAYAH, "to be," answering primarily to our old English word "to become," "to come about," "to begin to be or appear," either in time or space, is taken and used in the first person singular, future, twice, and so we have the proposition just cited,—"I will be, who I will be." This is the first affirmation.

Next, the first person singular future of this same verb HAYAH, "to be," namely, "I will be," is taken and used as a noun, and so becomes, "I who will be;" we have then this proposition,—"Thus shalt thou say to Israel's children,

I WHO WILL BE

hath sent me unto you." This is the second affirmation.

Finally, after this explanatory and emphatic introduction, we have the third person singular future, of the *old* form of this same verb HAYAH, "to be;" that old form, filled with Historic memories, recalling the last uttered longing of the dying Israel for the Deliverer yet to come, namely,

YAHVEH, HE WHO WILL BE,

reaffirmed in the instruction to Moses: "Thus shalt thou say unto Israel's children, 'YAHVEH,' (HE WHO WILL BE, 'the coming one,' 'the desired one,') God of your Fathers, the God of Abraham, the God of Isaac, and the God of Jacob, hath sent me unto you. This is my Name forever, and this is my Memorial unto all Generations."

It has been stated that in these propositions the *absolute future form* of the Hebrew verb "to be" is employed throughout.

The first affirmation, therefore, I WILL BE WHO I WILL BE, which introduces, and lends significance to the two succeeding statements, is a PROPHECY,—a prophecy uttered by no subordinate or delegated authority.

The expression here translated "I will be," is found in the first person singular *future*, of the Hebrew verb "to be," and signifies a FUTURE RELATION OF THE SPEAKER, in distinction from the Present or Past.

This first person singular, future, occurs *forty* times in the Hebrew Scriptures, and in every instance, whether in prose or poetry, exhibits the element of futurity,—a future relation of the speaker in action or conception.

It is repeated several times in this same chapter; we find it in History, Poetry, Prophecy, yet it is ever the same; the element of *futurity* is wrought into its very structure.

This fact has hitherto been utterly unknown to the general reader, in this connection. But that our English translation of this passage is not a *literal* rendering of the original, is well known to scholars.

Until, however, the discovery of the true derivation of "Jehovah," or YAHVEH, gave the clue to its meaning as a name, no motive existed for calling attention to the subject. Now the ancient Hebrew Scriptures, falling into the hands of philosophers rather than faithful students of History, bear the marks, to this day, of their speculations; giving us not the Historical YAHVEH, or "Jehovah," God of the Scriptures, but the philosophical "Theos," or "God" of Plato, and the school of Alexandria. This philosophical conception, beginning with the Septuagint, and endorsed by the Latin Vulgate, although departed from by Luther in his translation, has yet hitherto controlled the Theology of the World.

Other versions of the Scriptures, both ancient and modern, might show to the curious, that our English translation, in bringing forward the Septuagint "I am that I am," ran counter alike to ancient authority and Hebrew construction, in presenting an idea, familiar indeed to the Philosophers of Alexandria, but naturally foreign to the Hebrew mind, and for which, were such the thought intended, their language furnishes a specific formula.

These conclusions cannot be turned aside by ingenious reasoning on the nature and use of the Hebrew future in the abstract.

The forty witnesses to the future rendering of this form of the verb might be thought sufficient to establish it beyond question. But the case under consideration is stronger than any one of these. Here is a series of distinct propositions, independent of any context from which a doubt could by possibility be borrowed,—standing in an explanatory relation to each other,—the first two being used as introducing and reviving an old Historic term.

These propositions, then, must be judged by themselves, on their own literal merits. We find them all, in the simple absolute future.

Integrity of translation, therefore, requires not only the literal future rendering of these three affirmations, but also that the distinctions in the person of the verb, or between the introductory Prophecy and the Memorial Name, should be accurately set forth. Neither of these most important points have, as we have shown, been observed in our version. The English reader would naturally suppose the same form of the verb to be used throughout, in the original.

The knowledge however of the fact that this is not so, but that these propositions, all merged by our Translators in one form of statement, are distinct from, and explanatory of each other, ought to be enough to suggest to every thoughtful mind the possibility, that some important meaning may be involved in this extraordinary form of declaration.

What kind of interpretation is that, which, rejecting the future rendering of these propositions as unmeaning, though literal, would substitute the *present* throughout, thus ignoring every distinction of the original, on the plea that "*The self-existent*" is the most *suitable* name for God? Yet this is the principle adopted and expressed by "Johannes Damascenus," and the one which at a later period unfortunately controlled our Translators in rendering this passage.

Such a mode of interpretation, however, could only originate in a scholastic age. How many could be found at this day, who would consent thus to violate the truth of History, and the integrity of Criticism, by passing judgment upon any declaration of God, as *unsuitable*, and so blot from the Record this blazing Memorial of "YAHVEH," the DELIVERER?

But to return to the narrative: The name YAHVEH is not proclaimed as *new*. On the contrary, it is set forth as a Name which has had a *History*.

It is referred back to the God of Abraham, the God of Isaac, and the God of Jacob, and is affirmed as a Name replete with sacred associations, but at the same time as one whose Historical significance had become lost, and which was therefore explained, reasserted, and then given as a solemn pledge to the fulfillment of a Promise of Deliverance.

Thus Israel's children were to know, what

Israel himself had not known—YAHVEH as DELIVERER—they were also to "comprehend" more clearly, from their experience, and from the affirmation to Moses, that Name, as not only pledging Deliverance to them, but as prophetic of some great future manifestation to the world, of the same Person in a like relation.

The story of the Exodus is familiar to all. It is a story of the triumphs of YAHVEH, over the Magicians and Gods of Egypt.

Deliverance, Deliverance! breathes out from every line, and YAHVEH is the great DELIVERER.

YAHVEH destroys the Egyptians and "passes over" the dwellings of His people—and YAHVEH institutes the great feast of the "Passover"—to be perpetuated as a "memorial" together with His "memorial name" to all generations.

That great feast, to be called by the Israelites "YAHVEH'S Passover" is still observed throughout all Christendom, with a change, and yet a correspondence of emblems, in commemoration of the Deliverance of "Christ our Passover," and is called, "the Lord's Supper"—thus perpetuating the great "memorial" of

Israel's Deliverance from bondage,—and the yet greater DELIVERANCE foreshadowed in the prophetic name of YAHVEH.

So also the great and final act of YAHVEH in delivering His people from the power of the Egyptians, is commemorated in a song of Moses and the hosts of Israel, which song also is in Revelation, represented as sung by the redeemed hosts of Christ the Deliverer. "And they sing the song of Moses . . . and the song of the Lamb." The union, thus, of the song of Moses, with that of the Redeemed through Christ, is a union of the two great Historic Divisions of the Church in a common song of DELIVERANCE.

And DELIVERANCE is the grand representative idea of the Jewish system.

He who was to become the Theocratic Head of the nation, their Lawgiver and King, takes upon Himself the name of DELIVERER, and in illustration of that name, introduces His government by a glorious act of DELIVERANCE.

Thus in the History of Israel as a nation, prior to the relation of Law, is instituted the relation of *affection*—before the idea of the Lawgiver and the subject, comes that of Redeemer and Redeemed.

And this idea underlies the whole system. The name YAHVEH—the name which pledged and wrought DELIVERANCE, is a constant appeal to affectionate obedience, and a perpetually recurring pledge of peculiar watchfulness and care.

But the cause of YAHVEH, in the world as opposed to that of the great Enemy, has hitherto had no organized centre. The struggle has however been maintained and has silently progressed,—from family to family the record of the ancient Promise has been handed down, and with the record, a trust in the God of the Promise—step by step, the prophecy of the "Coming One" has unfolded itself, till thus, as we have seen, under the ancient name of the Promise, YAHVEH appears to Moses, explains and reaffirms that name, repeats the prophecy contained in it, and declares it to be His Memorial Name to all generations, and as if to unite forever the name YAHVEH, with the person "Elohim," "God"—the names are at first several times interchanged, after which "Elohim" is almost entirely dropped in the narrative, and YAHVEH, "Jehovah" is the Deliverer, the Redeemer; the Father and God of the Hebrew nation.

But the ever widening circle of YAHVEH's relation to Humanity, demands new revelations of Himself and new provisions for the exigencies of the struggle with the great Adversary. A nation is to be enlisted under the banner of YAHVEH, to stand as representative of His side of the contest in the world. That nation must be governed by a Law. It must also be educated for its great mission. It must be instructed in the eternal distinctions between "good" and "evil," "right" and "wrong," "sin" and "holiness." The lines between these opposing forces in the world must be distinctly drawn, with no compromise of boundaries—and these distinctions must be made plain and familiar, adapted to half-barbaric and childish minds, by striking and perpetually recurring ceremonials and types.

Accordingly, YAHVEH instructs Moses in a system of Law, wonderfully fitted to promote this great end,—a law, not only securing the outward prosperity of the nation, but following also each individual from day to day, and from hour to hour, with its pressure of individual responsibility to the Great Lawgiver.

Thus the Ceremonial Law had for its end the subordination of the whole heart and life to God, and this idea could have been implanted in the world in no other way than by numberless, incessant, and otherwise trivial rites and observances.

The process of the education of Humanity as a whole, on the plan of the Great Teacher, has been precisely, and *necessarily*, that through which every individual must pass in coming to the knowledge and love of Holiness.

He must *hate* "*evil*," before he can *love* "*good;*" and the strength of the one feeling is the measure of the other. So, before any positive love of good can be introduced into the Race, it must be educated to *aversion* from evil in every form.

Thus YAHVEH, the Deliverer from Evil, must awaken in His people a "*hatred of sin.*"

The great educational idea, then, upon which the Law for the Israelites was framed, was, "hatred of evil." Accordingly we find the Moral Law, instead of being summed up in abstract principles of positive duty, is set forth in connection with specified forms of evil, or sin, and before each, the great distinctive "Not,"—"Thou shalt not,"—thus training the mind through that perpetual watch-word of the Israelite, to a knowledge or recognition of "sin," and an aversion, or "turning away" from it.

The Law, then, in preparing the World for the reception of more spiritual ideas, and the comprehension of the principles and precepts of the Great Deliverer to come, was a "School-master," in the sense of "an instructor," "a leader of children," and not merely, as some have supposed, a disciplinarian in uninterrupted exercise of the rod, the very term "*Law*," in Hebrew, meaning "*instruction*."

But the Law must necessarily awaken in the mind of the transgressor, a sense of sin, or self-condemnation in view of sin, and parallel with transgression, throughout the great system, ran the provision of "sacrifice;" *sacrifice*, in which the suffering victim was looked upon as representing the relation of the transgressor to Law, was a ceremonial fitted not only to develop an intense abhorrence and deep conviction of sin, but also to lead the mind away from any idea of "self-righteousness" in view of the Law, and to entire dependence upon another.

Thus YAHVEH, the Lawgiver, Himself originated a ground of forgiveness, or of "Law-rightness," to the transgressor of His own Law, the legal representation of which, appears in the system of Sacrifices.

Dependence upon YAHVEH, therefore, as the originator of the Law, and the Author of a Deliverance from the penalty of transgression, through "sacrifice," together with the utter renunciation of self-dependence, and self-rightness, was the great lesson of the Law, to be written on the hearts of the nation, before they could be prepared for the coming of YAHVEH, and the substitution of the Spiritual idea for its material type.

But everywhere throughout this great system of Law, we find YAHVEH, or "Jehovah," appealing to His own Name as significant of a special and tender relation, and as containing associations fitted to affect the hearts of His people.

The peculiar emphasis with which this is done on several occasions, together with the connection in which it is declared, and the fact that it is always associated with the attributes of God, *in relation to Humanity*, all show that this Great Memorial name was not intended to express the mere preëminence of an absolute and Self-existent God, *apart from Humanity*.

It is not a name of Terror, or of Awe, but a name of *Relation*, expressing peculiarly the attributes of mercy and long-suffering of a God who has taken upon Himself the work of Deliverance and Redemption, and who pledges Himself by that name, in spite of the sins of His people (which He will not leave unpunished), to carry that work through to its final triumph.

In confirmation of this, hear the answer of

Yahveh to the prayer of Moses: "I beseech thee, show me thy glory." "And He said, I will make all my goodness pass before thee, and I will proclaim the name Yahveh before thee, . . . . . and Yahveh descended in the cloud, . . . and proclaimed the name Yahveh, and Yahveh passed by before him, and proclaimed Yahveh, Yahveh God, merciful and gracious, long-suffering, and abundant in goodness and truth, keeping mercy for thousands, forgiving iniquity and transgression, and sin, yet will not always leave unpunished."

The attributes here prominently set forth as the special characteristics of God under the name Yahveh, are those of *Mercy*, in relation to Humanity. And yet while Yahveh proclaims Himself as *forgiving*, He also under that name declares He will not always leave unpunished, but will hold His people responsible to a standard of Right and Holiness represented by the Law.

Especial prominence is also given to the Name Yahveh, in the first table of the Law, by the Commandment, "Thou shalt not take the name of YAHVEH thy God in vain, for YAHVEH will not hold him guiltless, who taketh His name in vain."

Thus YAHVEH, or "Jehovah," so wonderfully related to their History as a Nation, was to be regarded with peculiar reverence and affection, and he could not be held guiltless who profaned, by a light and empty use, so hallowed and significant a Name.

Out of this commandment, and another concerning the punishment of the blasphemer of the name YAHVEH, grew up at a later period among the formalistic Jews, a superstition which affects Christendom to this day.

It is well known, that after the Captivity, the Hebrew ceased to be spoken by the Jews, a corruption, called Syro-Chaldaic, taking its place. Paraphrases of the Scriptures written in this dialect, therefore, took the place of the ancient Hebrew among the people, who could understand the original only through an interpreting medium. The precepts of the Talmud, also, believed by the Jews to have been handed down directly from Moses by oral tradition, and to be of equal authority with the Law, were taken as interpreters both of the Paraphrase, and the Original.

These Talmudic commentaries on the sacred text, embody the grossest absurdities and puerilities. No other perversion, however, is equal to that suffered by the Ancient, Historic, the Memorial and Prophetic Name YAHVEH.

Witness the following declaration of the Talmud Sanhedr: "Etiam qui pronunciat nomen (Dei) suis literis, non est ei pars in seculo futuro." "Whoever utters the Name of God, (YAHVEH, or 'Jehovah,') with its own letters, hath no part in the world to come."

This was the superstition in the mind of Josephus when he wrote, "The name of God is a Name not lawful to be uttered." That a similar tradition prevailed with respect to the Law, or the "Ten Commandments," is shown by the further remark of Josephus in referring to these, "Which (he says) it is not lawful for us to write in their own words."

This latter superstition may be taken as a measure of the value of the former.

The very care to preserve and render significant the Law, and the Name of YAHVEH, was taken as the foundation of that formalistic perversion which emptied both of their meaning.

The dread of the punishment of the blasphemer caused the use of the name YAHVEH to be avoided among the Jews, and so after a while, they came to regard it as "too sacred" to be uttered, — as "the Ineffable Name," substituting for it in reading, as we have before stated, the vowels of another name of God, "Adonai," which "Adonai" has given us "the Lord" of our English version.

Thus this Great Name, given by God as a Memorial to all generations, — set forth as a *Name* of *Relation*, — appealed to as a name of *Affection*, — containing in its very structure and History a prophecy of Hope, — became, through a perversion of the very means taken to preserve its significance, completely extinct among the people to whom it was given.

And yet this wretched Jewish superstition, — one of those condemned by Christ in the woe pronounced upon the Pharisees for making *void* the Law through their *traditions*,—of which not a trace is to be found in the Sacred Record,—a part of that miserable perversion of the Majesty of the Ancient Ceremonials, which substituted blind and fatal formalism for glorious and living truths,—has been allowed by the Christian Church to cast its blighting shadow upon the History and the Name of YAHVEH.

This very superstition is not unfrequently adduced in confirmation of the rendering "I am that I am." Because the Jews regarded the Name "YAHVEH," or "Jehovah," with such so-called *suitable* veneration, it is inferred that this Name must express those attributes in which God is "afar off" from Man, and so becomes an object of awe and dread.

Superstition, and, in this connection, the false Philosophy of the Septuagint, with its preconceived Platonic idea of "Theos," or God, as "the Self-existent One," have thus combined to set their seal of death upon the glorious and living Name of YAHVEH.

But it cannot be holden of the bonds of

death. The time will come, prophesied by YAHVEH Himself to Moses, when this great and glorious Name shall fill the whole earth.

This prophecy is made to Moses by way of encouragement to him, in view of the sins of Israel, and as answering his appeal to the attributes of mercy and long-suffering set forth under the name YAHVEH.

Numbers XIV.: 21.

"And YAHVEH said, I have pardoned according to thy word, but truly as I live, all the earth shall be filled with the glory of YAHVEH."

The promise made to Abraham on the side of Humanity, that in his Seed should all the families of the earth be blessed, is thus reaffirmed to Moses on the side of Divinity, in the Promise that the Glory of YAHVEH shall fill the whole earth.

These two great Promises, concerning the Seed of Abraham, and the Person YAHVEH, or the Humanity and Divinity of the Coming DELIVERER, constitute the *germ*, of which the later and more specific declarations of the Prophets are but the development.

In the History of YAHVEH, the Coming DELIVERER, these two Promises, then, introduce the era of the Prophets "who spake of Him."

"In thy Seed shall all the families of the earth be blessed." And,

"Truly as I live, all the earth shall be filled with the glory of YAHVEH."

## CHAPTER VI.

### PROCLAIMED BY THE PROPHETS.

The dying words of David, the Sweet Psalmist of Israel, and the kingly representative of the Messiah, are recorded in 2 Sam. 23: 1—8.

This passage, containing, as may be shown on established authority, a direct and beautiful prophecy of the coming of Yahveh, as God and as Man, is yet so obscure in our version, as to be utterly meaningless to the ordinary reader.

It is impossible to follow this chapter as it stands in our Bibles, without a feeling of disappointment, in passing from the elevated strain in which the dying king calls attention to his words, and the words themselves, as they are set forth in the succeeding verses.

The number of interpolations by our Translators, shows that they could make no sense of the original, the text being to them inextricably confused. Since their time, however, other manuscripts have been discovered which throw great light upon this passage.

Upon the authority of the oldest and best of these,—the great reliance of Dr. Kennicott, his MS., No. 1,—YAHVEH, or "Jehovah," being restored to the text, is seen to be the "Sun" that "ariseth," and a prophecy at once appears, upon the discovery of which, Michaelis congratulates the critical and Christian world.

According to the critical text of Kennicott and De Rossi, following the arrangement, and mainly the version of the former, the passage reads thus:

TITLE.

Now these are the last words of David:

PROEM.

The oracle of David, the son of Jesse;
Even the oracle of the Man raised up on high
The Anointed of the God of Jacob,
And the Sweet Psalmist of Israel.

The Spirit of YAHVEH speaketh by me;
And His word is upon my tongue:
YAHVEH, the GOD of Israel sayeth;
To me speaketh the Rock of Israel:

SONG.

The JUST ONE ruleth among men!
He ruleth by the fear of GOD!
As the light of the morning ariseth YAHVEH;
A sun without clouds, for brightness;
And as the grass from the earth, after rain.
Verily thus is my house with GOD:
For an everlasting covenant hath He made with me,
Ordered in all things and sure:
For He is all my Salvation, and all my desire.
But the sons of Belial shall not flourish;
As a thorn rooted up shall be all of them:
For they cannot be taken by the hand.
And the man, who shall touch them,
Shall be filled with iron and the staff of a spear:
But with fire shall they be utterly consumed in their dwelling.

It will be seen that this passage thus arranged has the form of poetry. This is its proper form; Hebrew poetry consisting not in the rhythm of words merely, but of *ideas*, balanced against each other in *parallelisms*.

By parallelism is meant simply a repetition of the same, or a contrasted idea, in a rhythmical manner, by a balanced parallel statement; repetition or contrast thus adding force to the first idea.

Our Translators being ignorant of the nature of Hebrew poetry, have rendered it as if it were prose. Consequently all the beauty, and very much of the meaning, belonging in the original to the poetic form, is lost to us, from this defect of our version,—poetic statements full of significance, being often turned into quite incomprehensible prose.

A translation giving all the poetry of the Hebrew Scriptures in proper parallelisms, would bring out a world of meaning, and would startle and attract with something of the power and pressure of a new Revelation.

Isaiah proclaims the COMING of YAHVEH!

Isaiah XL.

A voice crying:—

In the wilderness, prepare ye a way for YAHVEH!
Make straight in the desert, a highway for our GOD!
Every valley shall be exalted, every mountain and hill
shall be made low;

And the crooked shall be made straight, and the rough places plain !
And the glory of YAHVEH shall be revealed,
And all flesh shall see it together:—
For the mouth of YAHVEH hath spoken.

* * * * * *

Oh Thou that tellest glad tidings to Zion, get thee up into the high mountain!
Oh Thou that tellest glad tidings to Jerusalem, lift up thy voice with strength!
Lift it up!——Be not afraid!
Say unto the cities of Judah, "Behold your GOD!"
Behold the sovereign YAHVEH shall come with strength!

* * * * * *

He shall feed His flock like a Shepherd:
He shall gather the Lambs with His arm, and carry them in His bosom:
And shall gently lead those that are with young.

The Law has now, in a measure, answered the purpose for which it was instituted. It has developed, in the world, through numberless transgressions, the idea of SIN.

The voices of the Prophets are lifted up in one prolonged wail over the iniquities of Israel, and with this great cry of "Sin!" "Sin!" comes the depreciation of the mere formal observance of the Ceremonial Law, and the proclamation of "The Coming One," as a DELIVERER from SIN.

Isaiah is filled with these two great ideas: "To what *purpose* is the multitude of your sacrifices unto me? saith YAHVEH. . . . I delight not in the blood of bullocks or of lambs, or of he-goats. . . . . Bring no more vain oblations! Incense is an abomination unto me! . . . Your appointed feasts my soul hateth, I am weary to bear them!" And in contrast with such formal observances it is spoken of the Coming One in another part of the prophecy:

"Surely it shall be said, In YAHVEH have I righteousness and strength."

Isaiah proclaims:

The UNIVERSAL TRIUMPH of YAHVEH!

IS. XLV.

I, YAHVEH, and no GOD beside me,
A just GOD, and a Saviour, none beside me,
Look unto ME and be ye saved,
All the ends of the earth,
For I am GOD, and none else.

I have sworn by MYSELF: the word is gone out of my mouth in righteousness,
And shall not return:
That unto ME every knee shall bow,
Every tongue shall swear.
Of ME it shall be said,
"Surely in YAHVEH is righteousness and strength;"
Unto HIM shall they come, and all who scorn HIM shall be confounded.
In YAHVEH shall all the seed of Israel be justified and shall glory.

Jeremiah proclaims:

## The DELIVERANCE of YAHVEH.

### Jer. XXIII.

Behold the days come, saith YAHVEH,
That I will raise up unto David a righteous Branch,
And a King shall reign and prosper,
And shall execute judgment and justice in the earth.
In His days Judah shall be saved,
And Israel shall dwell safely;
And this is HIS Name, whereby HE shall be called,
YAHVEH, OUR RIGHTEOUSNESS.
Therefore, behold the days come, saith YAHVEH,
That they shall no more say "As YAHVEH liveth,
Who brought up the children of Israel out of the land of Egypt!"

But "As YAHVEH liveth,
Who brought up and who led the seed of the house of Israel from the North Country,
And from all countries whither I had driven them!"
And they shall dwell in their own land!

Zechariah foretells:

The RECEPTION of YAHVEH.

Zech. XI.

"And I said unto them, If ye think good, give me my price, and if not, forbear. So they weighed for my price thirty pieces of silver.

"And YAHVEH said unto me, Cast it unto the potter: a goodly price that I was prized at of them!

"And I took the thirty pieces of silver and cast them to the potter in the house of YAHVEH."

Zech. XII.

. . Saith YAHVEH,
Who stretcheth forth the heavens,
And layeth the foundation of the earth,
And formeth the spirit of man within him,
* * * * *
* * * * *
They shall look upon ME whom they have pierced,
And shall mourn.

Isaiah predicts the effect upon the nation of their treatment of YAHVEH.

Is. VIII.

To YAHVEH of Hosts Himself, pay holy homage.
Even Him be your fear, and Him your dread;
And He shall be for a Sanctuary,
But for a Stone of Stumbling, and a rock of offence
To both houses of Israel;
For a gin and a snare
To the inhabitants of Jerusalem.
And many among them shall stumble,
And shall fall, and be broken,
And be snared, and be taken.

Malachi, the last of the Prophets, warns of the near approach of THE SOVEREIGN, YAHVEH Himself being Speaker.

Mal. III.

Behold I send my Messenger,
And he shall prepare the way before ME.
And THE SOVEREIGN whom ye seek, will suddenly come to HIS temple.
Even the Messenger of the Covenant, whom ye delight in,
Behold HE cometh, saith YAHVEH of Hosts.

The term SOVEREIGN in this passage is by Hebrew usage appropriated exclusively to the

Supreme God, and is in Exodus applied to YAHVEH, or "Jehovah," as "the Sovereign Jehovah, God of Israel."

It occurs eight times in the Old Testament, and has this application in each instance, admitting of no other.

Haggai shows that this SOVEREIGN is YAHVEH,—the DESIRE of all Nations.

### Haggai II.

For thus saith YAHVEH of Hosts,
It is yet a very little time,
And I will shake the heavens and the earth,
And the Sea, and the dry land;

And I will shake all Nations;
And the DESIRE of all Nations shall come,
And I will fill this house with glory;
Saith YAHVEH of Hosts.

Mine is the silver, and mine is the gold,
Saith YAHVEH of Hosts.

Great shall be the glory of this house,
The latter above the former;
Saith YAHVEH of Hosts.
And in this place I will give peace,
Saith YAHVEH of Hosts.

We have said that the great burden of the cry of the Prophets is, "Sin!" "Sin!" But it is not so much a transgression of the *Law*, as a transgression of the *relation of affection*, which they set forth. *Ingratitude* is the great crime of the People. The DELIVERANCE and the NAME of YAHVEH is constantly appealed to, and contrasted with the iniquities of Israel.

YAHVEH Himself mourns over this ingratitude, and pleads with His people. The prophecies are full of such passages. "Come now and let us *reason* together, saith YAHVEH."

"What more could have been done to my vineyard that I have not done in it?"

"I have nourished and brought up *children*, and they have rebelled against me."

"The ox knoweth his owner, and the ass his master's crib, but *Israel* doth not know, *my people* doth not consider."

"Oh earth, earth, earth, hear the word of YAHVEH!"

And yet though they have trampled upon the relation of DELIVERER in which YAHVEH has been "known" to them through all their

History as a nation, that name is still held out as a pledge and a prophecy of future DELIVERANCE from the bondage of SIN.

And now the coming DELIVERER is the great theme of Hope and prophecy, set forth in continual contrast with the dark citations of Israel's iniquity.

These transitions are found on every page of prophecy. Israel has trampled under foot the memory of the DELIVERANCE of YAHVEH, but YAHVEH will yet triumph in a nearer and more spiritual relation, not only over Israel, but over the whole Earth.

We have seen the prophecy to Abraham on the side of Humanity.

"In thy Seed shall all the families of the Earth be blessed."

And to Moses on the side of Divinity, "Truly as I live, the whole earth shall be filled with the glory of YAHVEH!"

Along the line of History, the prophecies of the Divinity, and of the Humanity of the Coming One, have hitherto stood in a measure apart.

The great work of the Prophetic Era appears to be the *interweaving* of these two ideas, as a preparation for the Coming of the Divine YAHVEH in the person of the Messiah.

We now find a continued series of statements concerning the Divinity and the Humanity of the Coming DELIVERER, so interchanging the personalities of the two, as to *identify*, beyond possibility of separation, or essential distinction, the two sets of prophecies as relating to *one person.*

"For unto us a child is born, unto us a SON is given." — "They shall call His Name IMMANUEL (God with us). He shall be called Wonderful, Counsellor, Mighty God, Father of Eternity, Prince of Peace."

Such passages, and those identifying the DELIVERER of the past with the DELIVERER to come, abound in, nay, may be said to *constitute* of themselves, the prophecies of the Old Testament.

The mind of the Prophet was filled with the conception of YAHVEH, — as upon the throne of the universe, — as walking the circle of the heavens,—as dwelling in the fullness of Glory.

From that central position, or point of conception, He is seen as about to interpose His own arm of Salvation, to bring DELIVERANCE to man.

Then he appears upon earth as "the Man of Sorrows," "stricken and afflicted," "despised and rejected," "acquainted with grief," "pierced," "making his grave with the wicked."

Again, bursting the bars of death, HE rises and reigns as Messianic King,—whose dominion is an everlasting dominion, which shall not pass away, and his Kingdom that which shall not be destroyed,—and in the full glory of whose reign, even upon the bells of the horses, shall be inscribed

HOLINESS TO YAHVEH.

# CHAPTER VII.

## COMPLETE IN CHRIST.

AND HE CAME. The long-expected DELIVERER, THE SOVEREIGN, came *suddenly* to His Temple, — yet heralded by Angels and proclaimed by His Messenger. He came to "His own," — "to the lost sheep of the house of Israel." He who had aforetime sent His prophets with "Thus saith YAHVEH," — Himself now brings the message of DELIVERANCE from SIN.

YAHVEH in the person of CHRIST speaks on earth.

YAHVEH, HE WHO WILL BE, becomes CHRIST, THE ANOINTED, THE MESSIAH. But the eyes of the nation are holden, that they know Him not.

His very name, veiled in superstition and

represented by a false and foreign word, is indeed "incommunicable" to their blinded hearts.

Yet, some among them receive and know Him. To this the Apostle John testifies.

John xii.

"These things said Esaias when he saw His Glory, and spake of Him" (Christ).

Now this is the Glory which Esaias saw.

Is. vi.

"I saw the Sovereign sitting upon a throne, high and lifted up! and His train filled the Temple. Above it stood the Seraphim, . . . and one cried unto another, saying,

"Holy, holy, holy, Yahveh of Hosts!

The whole earth is full of His glory!

"Then said I: Woe is me! for mine eyes have seen the King, Yahveh of Hosts!"

The above may stand as an illustration of the manner in which the New Testament writers refer to the Hebrew Scriptures as speaking of Christ.

To cite the numberless instances would be superfluous.

Their great aim appears to be to *identify* CHRIST, THE MESSIAH, with YAHVEH of the Old Testament.

Thus, they affirm:

That Isaiah saw the glory of CHRIST, and spake of Him.

In Isaiah it is the glory of YAHVEH.

That CHRIST was the leader of Israel in the wilderness.

In the narrative of their wanderings they were led by YAHVEH.

That Moses preferred the reproach of CHRIST to the treasures of Egypt.

In Exodus it is YAHVEH, for whom he endures all things.

That, at the giving of the Law, the voice of CHRIST shook the earth.

In Exodus it is the voice of YAHVEH.

That the spirit of CHRIST spake by the Prophets.

The Prophets themselves refer their utterances to the spirit of YAHVEH.

This breadth of reference in the New Testament writers to CHRIST, as pervading the History of the Old, cannot be explained on the ordinary view.

So also their references to passages in the Psalms and Prophets, as prophetic of CHRIST, appear often quite indiscriminate and incomprehensible on the narrow methods of interpretation prevailing at the present day in the Christian Church in respect to the CHRIST of Old Testament History.

And yet there is a strong under-current of feeling, that the mystery of CHRIST. as related to that History, is not solved.

The pressure of the facts above set forth,—the continual identification by the Apostles of the New Testament CHRIST, with the Old Testament YAHVEH,—has compelled the adoption by many, of the *theory* rather than the *belief* that the "Jehovah Angel" was CHRIST.

It is no new thing to assert that CHRIST appeared in the form of "the Jehovah Angel" to His ancient people.

It is safe to affirm, however, indeed it cannot be denied, that no distinction of *persons* can be maintained between "Jehovah" and "the Jehovah Angel" of the Old Testament, or between YAHVEH, and MALAK YAHVEH. They are continually interchanged, in such a manner as to exclude the possibility of distinction, except on the ground of "a manifested presence." As an instance, vide Ex. 3: 2—7.

When YAHVEH *appears* to man, or gives any *visible sign* of His presence, that visible sign or appearance, is called MALAK YAHVEH, or MESSENGER YAHVEH.

This "manifestation," "messenger," or "Angel," as a *man* walks and talks with Abraham, as an *Angel* wrestles with Jacob, communes face to face with Moses, is seen in the heavens by the Elders of Israel.

The pillar and the cloud also were the visible signs of YAHVEH'S presence to the Israelites in the wilderness, leading them in their wanderings; each was to them in turn, MALAK YAHVEH, and out of the glory and out of the cloud was heard the voice of YAHVEH, when He spake with Moses.

MALAK YAHVEH, then, is the first manifestation of YAHVEH to Humanity, and the preparation for that more wonderful revelation of Himself to the world, as THE MESSENGER of THE NEW COVENANT, of which great future manifestation, the name YAHVEH is itself a Prophetic MEMORIAL.

Not only in this *special* manner do the Apostles assert the identity of CHRIST with YAHVEH, but they assume that identity as an established fact, by attributing to CHRIST, in His final coming and Kingdom, all the glory and dominion everywhere throughout the Old Testament ascribed to YAHVEH.

The arguments also, by which they established the Divinity of the man CHRIST JESUS, are always Historical arguments.

Beginning at the Creation, they affirm that the same Being who laid the foundations of the earth, and who manifested Himself to the ancient Church from time to time along the line of its History, appeared in the person of CHRIST on earth.

They do not begin with His Humanity, and add on names and attributes to prove Him

Divine. They *begin* with His Divinity, which Divinity, or Divine Personality, they declare superintended the world from the Beginning, manifested itself from time to time in History, and finally appeared on Earth as THE MESSIAH.

In the Apostolic view, then, the manifested presence of CHRIST began at the very foundation of the Church, — the transient and varying forms by which He appeared to His ancient people, preparing them for the more permanent and universal manifestation of Himself in the person of the great MALAK YAHVEH — CHRIST, THE MESSIAH.

Thus, they declare in the most absolute manner, the identity of YAHVEH, the Founder of the Jewish Church, with CHRIST, the Great High Priest, who, by the sacrifice of Himself, abolished the merely legal and representative ordinances, and completed the Dispensation which He instituted.

This Completed Dispensation, is set forth in the New Testament, as a great Historic Fact and Unit containing from beginning to end the revelation of the work of CHRIST in the world, no one part of which can be comprehended without the other, and of which, *One Divine Person,* under the successive names, YAHVEH and CHRIST, constitutes the sublime unity.

But here it may be asked, If these things are so, where is the Doctrine of the Trinity? The relation of Father and Son? Of God, and Mediator between God and man?

Before this question can be answered, it is necessary to set forth the distinctions everywhere preserved in the original of the Hebrew Scriptures in the names of God, no shadow of which distinction appears in our Translation.

We find three great names used by the Old Testament writers.

ELOHIM, ADONAI, and YAHVEH, or "Jehovah." These names, as we have said, are everywhere distinct in the original, yet interchange under the relations of the work of Deliverance and Redemption.

ELOHIM and YAHVEH are the two distinctive names of the Old Testament. ADONAI, "Sovereign," is a title expressive of Governmental Relation, and takes the place of either ELOHIM or YAHVEH, according to the circumstances, or the feeling of the writer.

ELOHIM, " God," "whom no man hath seen at any time," a name infolding *all* the attributes of *God*, as opposed to *man*, stands "in the Beginning," as CREATOR of the universe.

" In the Beginning ELOHIM created the heavens and the earth."

This ELOHIM is a remarkable word. It is the title of THE ONE GOD, as contrasted with Polytheistic ideas.

Yet this term is a plural noun, appearing everywhere as the subject or nominative of verbs in the singular. This noun, standing thus in the plural number, and nominative to verbs in the singular, is also used as infolding distinct personalities, as in this remarkable case:

" And ELOHIM said, Let us make man in OUR image, according to OUR likeness."

YAHVEH, or YAHVEH ELOHIM, is a name of RELATION. It is a name, as we have shown, growing out of the expectation of Humanity, in view of a Divine Promise.

He who gave the promise, adopted its name, and entered into a relation of *Affection* with the Race.

This name, originating in *human* want and need, having a *human* History and growth, and yet representing a Divine Promise, was fitly chosen as foreshadowing the incarnation of the Divine person who assumed it to Himself, and proclaimed it as His MEMORIAL NAME.

YAHVEH ELOHIM also assumes all the attributes of ELOHIM, and makes use in two instances of the plural form to which we have alluded:

"And YAHVEH ELOHIM said, 'Behold the Man is become as one of us, to know good and evil.'

"And YAHVEH said, . . . 'Let us go down, and there let us confound their language.'"

Thus ELOHIM by derivation and use is a term expressive of POWER, and represents the Object of Awe and Reverence, standing at the Head of the Universe.

ADONAI, "Sovereign," expresses a relation of DOMINION.

Yahveh represents a relation of Deliverance and Affection.

We are now prepared to consider Historically the questions before asked:

In this view where is the Doctrine of "the Trinity?" The relation of "Father" and "Son?" Of "God," and "Mediator between God and man?"

The Historic facts with respect to the Divine Personalities set forth in the Scriptures are these.

Elohim, the God of Power, appears first as Creator, and in speaking, uses a form of expression implying the existence of other Personalities on an equality with Himself.

Yahveh Elohim enters into relation with man, assumes all the attributes of Elohim, and maintains a special superintendence over the Race.

Yahveh Elohim also uses the plural form in speaking, implying the existence of other Personalities on an equality with Himself.

And yet these names are continually interchanged in such a manner as to produce the impression of *Unity*.

Coming to the Psalms and the Prophets, however, the distinctions are more apparent.

Two Divine persons are represented—sometimes *The One*, as commissioning, sending, and sustaining *The Other*, who is looked upon as *sent*.

More often, however, the Divine Speaker identifies with Himself a Person invested with all the attributes of Divinity, who is represented as a suffering Messiah, and also as a Triumphant and reigning King.

The ground for distinction in personalities is thus laid in the Old Testament.

Except for the comparatively few instances, however, in which a Divine Speaker, *other* than YAHVEH ELOHIM appears, YAHVEH is "*the One God*" of the Hebrew Scriptures.

That other Speaker, "whom no man hath seen at any time," stands in a relation to the Old Testament YAHVEH as sending Him, and sanctioning His work, like that of the "Father" in the New Testament, to "the Son."

In the course of the Prophecies, when YAHVEH

ELOHIM is looked upon as "leaving heaven," and so as in a measure "parted off" from the full glory of Divinity, the name YAHVEH is, in a few instances, assumed by another Divine Speaker, who takes the place of YAHVEH in the heavens, and by adopting His name, expresses His own participation in the work of Deliverance and Redemption, at the same time, maintaining in the world, the idea of a Divine Deliverer still at the Head of the Universe.

When YAHVEH appears upon Earth as THE MESSIAH, and by His incarnation becomes "our elder brother," He bears another Name, CHRIST "The Anointed," and is called "The Son."

A joint interest in the one object of the economy of this world is also in the New Testament expressed by the terms "Father" and "Son" as distinctive of the Divine personalities engaged in the work, as in the Old Testament that idea is conveyed by an interchange of the Name of the Deliverer, YAHVEH.

We have seen the origin and History of the Name YAHVEH, in the Old Testament.

We have alluded also to Superstition and

false Philosophy, as so blinding the hearts of the Jewish nation, that when the great MESSIAH, YAHVEH, in the person of CHRIST, appeared on earth, they knew Him not.

YAHVEH, the original Name of the Promise, being veiled in Superstition, and its meaning lost, we find the Expectation of the World represented by a new term.

The Hebrew people now (before the Coming of CHRIST), in common with the rest of the civilized world, have adopted a new language.

In that language, which, spreading from the great centre of Ancient Philosophy and Art, merged all nationalities in one common tongue, *The Expectation of the World* is represented by a term, adapted through the medium of this universal language to the comprehension not of *one* nation only, but of the whole world.

This term is in familiar use as representing the expected MESSIAH.

It is a Greek word, the precise equivalent of the old Hebrew YAHVEH, and its Historical origin and growth are in a measure parallel.

Ho ERKOM'ENOS (The Coming One, or He

who is to Come) represents again not the expectation of a *Nation*, but of the world.

Thus, John, hearing the fame of Jesus, sent unto Him two disciples, with this question:

"Art thou 'Ho Erkom'enos' (The Coming One), or look we for another?"

We shall find this term adopted by the risen Saviour, and given through John, in Revelation, as a watchword to His Church, directing their expectation again, to His Second Coming.

Thus the promise of the Ancient Name Yahveh having been fulfilled, another term in another language has arisen, to be adopted and proclaimed to the world, as the equivalent of the Memorial Name Yahveh, the design of both being to keep alive in the mind the great idea, "Behold, I come! Watch!"

We have seen the foundation for a distinction of Personalities, laid in the very beginning of the Old Testament, gradually becoming more and more developed, till in the New Testament it is made prominent in the relation of "Father" and "Son."

Throughout the Epistles the distinction is in

a great measure preserved by the terms "Theos," "God," and "Kurios," "Lord," as applied to "Father" and "Son;" "Theos," however, often standing for the plural Personality. "Kurios" is also sometimes interchanged with "Theos." Almost uniformly, however, throughout the New Testament it is a term applied to CHRIST.

It is a little remarkable that the term "Lord," through the *Greek* of the Old and New Testaments, is made to represent first YAHVEH, and then CHRIST, if there is no design of identifying the two.

For, from the very Beginning to the End, "CHRIST" is thus made to appear as "Kurios," "Lord," to the glory of God the "Father."

The necessary inference from the foregoing Historical investigation seems to be the following:

He who appears in the New Testament as "God" the "Father," and of whom CHRIST declares: "No man hath seen God at *any* time, the only begotten Son, who is in the bosom of the Father, He hath declared Him," who in the epistles is spoken of as "Theos," *nowhere in the Old Testament appears as a distinct Personality, save as appointing and sanctioning the work of* YAHVEH ELOHIM.

YAHVEH, or YAHVEH ELOHIM, enters into relation with man,—walks with him in the Garden,—communes with the Patriarchs,—delivers from bondage,—proclaims the Law,—sends His Prophets,—comes to His own,—is rejected and crucified,—ascends into glory,—and will come again to judge the quick and the dead.

Zech. XII.

* * * * * "Saith YAHVEH,
Who stretcheth forth the heavens,
And layeth the foundations of the earth.
* * * * * *
They shall look upon ME, whom they have pierced
And shall mourn."

Revelation, 1: 7—11; 22: 13.

"Behold He cometh with clouds! and every eye shall see Him, and they also which pierced Him, and all kindreds of the earth shall wail because of Him: . . . . . I am Alpha and Omega,—the Beginning and the End,—the First and the Last,—He who IS, and who WAS, and (HO ERKOM'ENOS) who IS TO COME; the Almighty (Heb. EL SHADDAI)."

Here CHRIST announces Himself as EL SHADDAI, "the Almighty,"—as Alpha and Omega, the Beginning and the End, the First and the Last, who began of Old the work of the world's Redemption, and who will complete that work at the final Judgment.

These terms standing thus at the close of a completed Revelation of the work of Redemption, bringing together in *one* person, *all* the names under which the Divine Nature had revealed itself to man from the very beginning of that work to its end, seem emphatically to enforce the interpretation, to the exclusion of any other, that the speaker, CHRIST, is the *only Person* who has taken upon Himself that work, from the Beginning to the End of Time.

The idea prevailing among commentators that the proposition, "Who IS, and who WAS, and who IS TO COME," is to be metaphysically interpreted as expressing "Eternity of Being," is founded solely upon the supposition that it is the Apocalyptic expansion of the "I am" interpretation of the name "Jehovah," or YAHVEH, in Ex. 3: 15.

But this rendering of the name YAHVEH has been shown to be without foundation either in Exegesis or History.

Consequently the passage under consideration must be looked at as standing by itself.

In so considering it, we find that the *very terms of the proposition* exclude the metaphysical rendering, since the Greek would require "who is, and who was, and who *will be*," instead of "who IS, and WHO WAS, and who WILL COME," HO ESOM'ENOS, instead of HO ERKOM'ENOS,—as appears from the usage of Clemens Alexandrinus, in his comments upon the name "Jehovah,"—from the inscription on the Saïtic Temple of Isis, mentioned by Plutarch,—and from the well-known formula expressing the eternity of Jupiter, quoted by Pausanias,—in all of which HO ESOM'ENOS, or its equivalent, stands as the last clause of the proposition.

The New Testament use of the verb, "to come," needs no discussion.

It appears from these references that "Eternity of Being" was an idea familiar to the mind of Paganism as expressing its Philosophic conception of a *Great First Cause;* as such it may be said to be a "*necessary*" idea of the mind.

There is a natural tendency in the speculative religious mind to "*abstract*" from the idea of God all qualities relating Him to man.

The *whole aim* of Revelation, apart from the "I am" interpretation of Ex. 3: 15, appears to be, to *counteract* this tendency by presenting the idea of a God, *in relation to Humanity.*

It is certainly reasonable to suppose, therefore, that He who took upon Himself the "form of a man," would also reveal Himself under the limitations of *time* as related to the duration and destiny of the world He came to save.

We have stated that Ho ERKOM'ENOS was in familiar use as representing a *Coming* MESSIAH.

As such it is adopted by CHRIST as the watch-word of His Second Coming.

YAHVEH, the Promise of the First Coming, is fulfilled, and yet YAHVEH, the Memorial Name, still remains in its equivalent Ho ERKOM'ENOS.

Thus YAHVEH, "Jehovah" (He who will Be) of old, came according to His promise.

He WAS, and IS, and to us still HE IS TO COME.

He is to us YAHVEH (He who will Be).

He is, Ho ERKOM'ENOS (He who will Come).

Of Ho ERKOM'ENOS it is written:

"Behold He cometh with clouds, and every eye shall see Him!"

Even so, — Come, — YAHVEH JESUS!

# CHAPTER VIII.

## A NEW CHRISTOLOGY.

CHRISTOLOGY is *the Scriptural doctrine of the Person and Kingdom of* CHRIST.

Hitherto, human interpretation of the Divine teaching in respect to the person and work of THE DELIVERER, has left much of that teaching an unexplained mystery.

As we have shown, it fails to account for the manner in which the New Testament writers refer to the Hebrew Scriptures as enforcing the claims and explaining the work of CHRIST.

There is an unhesitating freedom and boldness, also, in their citations of passages, as containing Messianic predictions, which sometimes even an ingenious spirit of accommodation finds hard to harmonize with the present narrow and fragmentary views of the Christology of the Old Testament.

The facts presented in the foregoing pages, however, give a new aspect to that science.

In their light, CHRIST is seen to be "the beginning" as well as the "ending," "the Alpha" as well as the "Omega," of the World's History.

Thus Revelation becomes a sublime and simple story of THE DELIVERER, and of his work in the world, from the first to the second Paradise; the Unity of the Divine and majestic drama being found in the Person of the Deliverer, and the End for which He wrought.

In view of a Unity like this, the mind cannot vacillate in respect to the object of its faith and worship, as it is prone to do, in conceiving of the government and care of the world, as transferred, at a particular time, from one Divine person to another.

That God "the Father" should have been the special superintendent of an introductory, and therefore subordinate portion of the Divine scheme, and at a given time should have retired from such relation to the race, is a view, to say the least, appearing to fail in that unity which the mind naturally craves. It seems, also, out of harmony with the exaltation by Christ of "the Father," as inapproachable, save through Him "who is the brightness of His glory, and the express image of His Person," and to whom all power is given in Heaven, and upon Earth.

A not uncommon conception of "the Father," is that of "the God of the Old Testament" as Lawgiver, in a state of continued anger toward the Human Race, in consequence of their transgression of "the Law."

This state of anger, being insensibly transferred from the violation of the law as a *cause*, to the character of the Lawgiver, as an *inherent attribute* of that character, He is conceived of as only "placable" through Christ, who as a propitiating Mediator redeems and saves the otherwise lost world.

Thus between "Christ" and "the Father," a "diversity" is necessarily supposed to exist, adapting each to His own peculiar relation of

"Lawgiver" and "Mediator," and to the extent of that diversity a unity becomes impossible.

So long then as two Divine persons are conceived of as dividing the history of the world, representing, the one, "condemnation," and the other, "forgiveness," it is hardly possible to see in either separately "all the fullness of the Godhead," since the union of both ideas in *one person* seems essential to that conception.

This Partition of the Divine scheme, with its two representatives, may account in a measure for the contempt into which the Old Testament has fallen in some quarters, although it is difficult to see how any candid student of its history can find only "a *Jehovah* jealous and angry," even under the old view of that Name.

How utterly different, however, how sublime and overwhelming the interest which pervades its pages, when it is seen to be the Revelation of YAHVEH THE DELIVERER!—of HIM, "who now once, in the end of the world (literally, Dispensations), hath *appeared*, to put away sin by the sacrifice of Himself."

Revelation studied thus *Historically* rather than *Doctrinally*, becomes, from Genesis to the Apocalypse, all order, progress, and consistency.

The course of preparation, the mode of manifestation, and the character displayed by the Divine Superintendent of the Jewish Economy, is seen to be wonderfully adapted to precede and introduce the Great Historic Fact of His Incarnation.

Having revealed Himself as "Divine," as "God," He at last, in completing that dispensation, stands upon Earth, and declares, that He "came down from heaven," to manifest "the Father" unto men.

This declaration of "the Father" by Christ, is the highest and the latest phase of Revelation, and the one, for the reception of which, the world, from its very foundation, had been in a course of training.

How out of harmony with "the Father," as thus revealed by Christ, is the "*I am that I am*" rendering, given to the declaration in Exodus!

And yet, upon this very interpretation hangs

the whole doctrine of the God of the Old Testament as differing in character from the Christ of the New. This taken away, all else is beautifully consistent. YAHVEH appears everywhere the CHRIST of the Old Testament. Not even the tenderness of John exceeds that of Moses and Isaiah in declaring the word of YAHVEH.

So also the character of Christ as Judge, in his stern condemnation of persistent wickedness, is in perfect keeping with that of the Lawgiver and Ruler of Israel of Old, who by the mouth of His prophets uttered woe against all workers of iniquity.

Again: The Kingdom of Christ as set forth by the Apostles is identical with that proclaimed by the Prophets as the future Kingdom of YAHVEH.

Without attempt at explanation, or hint at any species of accommodation, they transfer to CHRIST all the predictions inevitably associated in their minds with the Kingdom of YAHVEH.

In the *Apocalypse* the veil is lifted from the last act of the great drama of the struggle between the Powers of Good and Evil. The

DELIVERER triumphant is seen crushing the head of the Great Adversary, the *Old Serpent*, who in putting forth his utmost efforts, but wounds the heel of his Victor.

To find an explanation of this Apocalypse, we are driven to the very first chapters of the Old Testament, where we see the first Act of the Drama recorded, and the two Opponents introduced, whose struggles for ascendancy constitute the unity of the intervening history.

The very last chapters of the Apocalypse, as if to perfect this Unity, return to the images of the first Paradise, "the Garden," "the Tree of Life," in the description of the restored Paradise, in view of which restoration, also, the Church of the Redeemed is represented as calling upon Ho ERKOM'ENOS (He who will Come) to come quickly, even as outside the first Paradise, the ancient world called upon YAHVEH (He Who will Be) to come and restore.

Indeed the whole Apocalypse may be looked upon as a prophetic expansion and fulfilment of the first great Messianic prediction or Promise:

"He shall crush thy head and thou shalt wound His heel."

Could any Unity be more perfect,—more transcendently divine?

And how can it be accounted for, on any other supposition than that of a Revelation, Divinely superintended from the very beginning to its close?

In this unity of the Historic facts of Revelation, there is a vitality and power, fitted to awaken enthusiasm in the most indifferent, and to fill with hope the most desponding.

If new life is to be infused into the present apparently torpid phase of Christianity, and we know new life *must* be infused before it can triumph in the struggle with the powers of darkness and of this world, it will come, we believe, so far as human agency is concerned, through a more thorough apprehension and exhibition of *Historic unity*, in the purposes and acts of the Divine Leader and Conqueror in that struggle.

That the identification of the *Lawgiver* with the *Mediator* as *one person*, appeals more potently to the affections than any other view, cannot be denied.

It also bridges over the great gulf generally conceived to exist between the Old and New Testaments.

He who talked with Adam, and made a covenant with Abraham, having instructed His people through "the Law" (TORAH, or "Law," in Hebrew meaning "instruction"), and having filled out the Spirit of that Law in person upon earth as an example of "the good" as opposed to "the evil,"—DIED,—that He might become the Captain of a Redeemed Host, "and unto them who look for Him, He will appear the second time, without sin, unto salvation."

The two dispensations are thus formed into a connected whole, of which *the one* is introductory to, and completed by *the other*,—the great central fact of the world's History,—the Death of Christ,—fulfilling all the types, and dispelling the shadows, of the first prophetic division of the great economy of Redemption.

With a perception of the demands of the Law, in the light of a Unity like this, comes a spontaneous recognition of the fact that we are "not under *Law*, but under *Grace;*" that He who *condemns*,—Christ our Judge,—"is Christ that *died*, yea, rather that is risen again, who is even at the right hand of God, who also maketh intercession for us."

The Law is thus impressed with tenfold force through the principle of *Love*.

But the life-giving power of this view lies preëminently in the fact, that it presents the God of History as a *Personal Being*.

The Affections demand a *personal* object. They cannot be moved by abstractions,—but only as they *are* moved can Christianity make progress. God as a personal Being, then, related to the race, and acting in History, is the proper object of affection.

In this mode of presentation there is a way to the hearts of men which, on principles of mental analysis, can be shown to be open in no other direction.

These principles have been already indicated: namely, that "*the affections*" demand a *personal object*, while "the *Intellect*," from its very nature, can nave for its object only "*abstractions.*"

In this simple, but broad distinction we may find the reason for a prevalent skepticism in regard to the God of History.

The tendency of mere Intellectual culture being to keep "the Intellect" in advance of "the affections," the affections become in a measure dormant, and the want of a *personality* upon which to fasten, or of God as a *Father of Spirits,* is not felt, while God, as a *Great First Cause,* is acknowledged to be a philosophic necessity.

The Intellect therefore substitutes its own object, an abstraction, and so the mind, divorced from the heart, sees enthroned at the head of the universe, not a *person* but a *Law.*

Hence the real doubt, or practical oblivion and denial of the works of the God of History, His workings being the outgoings of an intelligent plan, outlined and unfolded by a Personal Actor.

The Intellect, with its enthroned abstraction,

or "Law," disguised, but not altered in nature by being called a person, finds no such Personal Actor in its generalizations.

Miracles, therefore, or any disturbing interruptions of whatever may have been exalted into assumed Historic Law, are felt to be discomposing, uncalled for, not to say absurd; and so the Philosopher, speculating God out of History, and kneeling to some "absolute idea" of his own making, becomes practically atheistic.

A true mental culture, however, finds no such dreary end. Giving to the affections their due place, it demands in History a personal God. It perceives that want satisfied in Revelation. The affections coinciding with the perception result in Faith, or a practical belief in a personal God.

Faith then becomes to the mind, what sight is to the eye, — it holds the affections to their true object, puts reality for abstractions, and restores to History her exiled King.

Thus, the Believer, and not the Skeptic, is the true Philosopher.

The Divine Head of the Church has been *one* throughout all ages.

Here, then, is the basis of a true Catholicity, and the rallying point for divided sects:—"One Lord," the DELIVERER in the Old, and the REDEEMER in the New Dispensation;—"One Faith," in His Deliverance and Redemption,—"One Baptism," into His Death, and to the mighty and all embracing "Name" of "Father, Son, and Holy Spirit;"—the "One God and Father of all," whom He has revealed—ELOHIM,—who, in the Beginning, created the heavens and the earth, "who is above all, and through all, and in us all."

Thus we have a complete unfolding of the plural Personality and Divine Unity of ELOHIM—GOD—of that great and solemn Name, which, with its infolded attributes, stands in an opening Revelation, at the head of the Universe—a Name of power, of distance, and of mystery.

How has this revelation been effected? Through what process of training have the great facts of a Divine Incarnation, and the

Fathership of ELOHIM been wrought into the mind of the Race?

That which no human mind could conceive as possible, has been accomplished through the Mediatorship of Him "who was in the Beginning with God, and who was God." HE who thus was ELOHIM, taking upon Himself the name of the promise,— YAHVEH,— "He Who will Be," with which name was associated in the minds of the Fathers of the Race, the expectation of a Human Deliverer, revealed Himself to man under the prophetic Name

YAHVEH ELOHIM,

thus uniting the two ideas:

YAHVEH and ELOHIM.

HUMAN DELIVERER and GOD.

The Divine Person thus uniting in Himself these two ideas, by repeated manifestations, declarations, and prophecies, first of the one, or the side of Divinity, and then of the other, or the side of Humanity, and again by a union of the two, prepared the world to receive the wonderful Fact of a Divine Incarnation.

These alternations of a Divine personal

manifestation, throughout the first ages of the world, are constant, and rapidly successive.

YAHVEH appears in a human form, and enters into familiar intercourse with man,—again ascending, He speaks from Heaven as God,—descending, again makes Himself known by some visible, tangible token of His presence. These manifestations being accompanied from time to time, by Messianic declarations or promises, becoming at every step more and more distinct.

As the world advances, Prophecy, broadening and unfolding, takes the place of that personal intercourse, by means of which YAHVEH led by hand the early childhood of the Race, and He who was the friend of Abraham, then the Deliverer of Israel, rises into the Universal Sovereign of the Prophets, arrayed against wickedness, promising a personal interposition in behalf of man, and declaring for Himself a universal triumph in the end, over all opposing forces of evil.

This full assumption of Divinity, throughout the era of the Prophets, precedes and introduces that greatest of all manifestations of YAHVEH, — His appearance in the world as the long-looked for Human Deliverer, — CHRIST, — the MESSIAH, — who, coming as MAN, yet declared Himself GOD, asserting the Fathership of ELOHIM, — GOD, — of whose glory He Himself had been partaker, and from whom He proceeded forth, — who came explaining the nature of that kingdom destined to prevail upon earth, and claiming it as His own; — who, having conquered SIN, and that "last enemy," DEATH, thus delivering those "who through fear of Death, were all their lifetime subject to bondage," — returned to His Heavenly place, to His Father's House, to the fellowship of ELOHIM, leaving His followers, from whom He ascended, gazing upward after Him into Heaven, lost in the contemplation of His Glory.

But while they thus looked steadfastly upward, behold two men stood by them in white apparel, who also said:

"Ye men of Galilee, why stand ye gazing up into heaven? This same Jesus who is taken up from you into heaven, shall so come in like manner as ye have seen Him go into Heaven."

From that moment, the Divinity, or essential Deity, of the Lord and Saviour Jesus Christ, is their all-absorbing thought, and their controlling and inspiring theme.

From that moment also, not knowing "the times and the seasons," they are constant watchers for that "coming again" of the risen Saviour, foretold by the men in white apparel, which future personal manifestation would be the signal of the triumphant completion of His work.

But the Revelation to John in the Isle of Patmos sets the final seal of Divinity upon the human life of Jesus, and unites with the central ELOHIM, — GOD, — that lowly Saviour who had walked with His disciples on earth.

There He is beheld as the "Ancient of Days" seen in the vision of Daniel, as God Almighty, the Lamb in the *midst* of the Throne, as the final Judge of all the world, whose voice once shook the earth, and once again will shake not the earth only, but the heavens, — and who leaves with His Church the parting watchword:

"Behold I come quickly!"

In the Apocalypse also, the central ELOHIM, "Theos" or God,—in relation to "the Redeemed," is spoken of under the attributes of the Mediator, even as the Mediator upon earth assumes the attributes of ELOHIM,—GOD.

And the Mediator is revealed as reassuming His place at the Head of the universe in returning to the central ELOHIM, or GOD.

For the LAMB is seen in the MIDST of the Throne—even the "Great White Throne" of ELOHIM, of "Theos,"—of God—from which, and from the face of HIM that sitteth thereon, the earth and the heaven flee away, before whom also the Judgment is set, and the books are opened.

So "we shall all stand before the Judgment seat of CHRIST,"—who thus is ELOHIM,—who also is our SAVIOUR, and the Head of the Church.

The Divinity, or essential Deity of Jesus Christ ought then to fill the mind of His

Church as it did that of the Apostles after His ascension, and His last words, spoken from *Heaven* should be the fixed point of thought and expectation, from which to look back upon His life on earth, and forward to His Promised Coming.

And yet the supernatural facts in the History of Jesus should not so absorb the mind as to exclude the earnest and diligent study of His perfect life and example upon earth; for, in this respect He came to be the Light of the World,—to teach the brotherhood of man under the Fathership of ELOHIM,—day by day, humbly, patiently, perfectly, He did the will of that Father whose Son He became, by becoming the "elder brother" of Humanity.

This wonderful and beautiful life of Jesus upon earth, thus presents to man a Divine ideal for study and imitation.

So noble and exalted is this study, so wide is the field, and so manifold are the forms in which the principles of His Divine beneficence may be, nay, *must* be applied by His followers, that there has always existed in the Church, side by side with the opposite tendency, an element of *Humanitarianism*, or a tendency toward the too exclusive contemplation of the mere Humanity of Jesus, — in other words, to *works* without *faith*,—the extreme of which is a denial of the Divinity of Christ, or of a personal God in History; and as a consequence, the exaltation of the Individual Man as the centre of his own moral life, and the source of his own strength in the conflict with evil.

Such mortal armor, however, will not avail, for now, and always, as in the days of the Apostles, "we wrestle not with flesh and blood, but against principalities, against powers, against the rulers of the darkness of this world, against wicked Spirits on high," whose Leader is the Great Adversary, whom only "the whole armor of God" can withstand.

In such a conflict, therefore, the feebleness of unaided man, becomes often at the very outset, discouraged, and sinks easily into Indifferentism, or practical Atheism.

Again, on the other hand, there exists always in the Church, a tendency in the opposite direction — or to such an exclusive maintenance of the doctrine of the essential Deity of the Saviour, and of His atoning Death, as almost loses sight of that part of His Mediatorial work involved in His life and example upon earth, — in other words, to a "faith without works," which being "dead," or without fruit, tends to Formalism, the extreme of which is Superstition, and carried into action, becomes Fanaticism.

Thus to the *incompleteness* of either view, according as the one has prevailed in the Church to the exclusion of the other, may be traced the rise and progress of the opposite errors.

Yet such are the limitations of the human mind, and so infinite the breadth of a true Historic Christianity, that it can hardly be wondered at that the History of the Church has presented an alternation of these phases.

The latter, or Theistic, as opposed to the Humanitarian phase of Christianity, prevails in times of trouble and persecution, when the Rulers of the darkness of this world hold sway, and appear to have triumphed,—then the Church is driven to call upon a Divine Deliverer, and delights to behold in the Saviour a personal God, who has pledged Himself to be its leader in a final triumph over the Powers of Evil.

In such times, also, the Church, (by which is meant, of course, *the working leaven* of Christianity in every age,) being shut out from activity in the world, becomes essentially Theistic, and is characterized by great individual zeal and fervor of piety. When, however, the pressure is removed, and the exigencies of the times demand new duties, if it continue in narrow individualism, and refuse to meet the new duties of an altered position, persistently holding itself aloof from the great questions of the age and of Humanity,—then, to the extent of that dereliction, its leaven departs, and it becomes inevitably superseded by some other phase of a Church never dying, but ever struggling towards a complete Christianity.

The former, or Humanitarian phase, is developed in times of peace, or of widely diffused outward prosperity.

Religion, then, losing, in a great measure, its contemplative character, occupies itself with works of private beneficence, or schemes of extended philanthropy. Becoming objective, eager, restless, and enterprising, it inclines to take "the principles of Christianity" as a motto of *reform*, rather than Christ as a personal guide, and tends to become *a Christian philanthropy*, rather than a true Christianity.

Aiming, also, to develop and ennoble every faculty of man, it enters into each department of life, and seeks to bring under its influence all that appeals to him as an intellectual and moral being.

In so doing, it is open always to the great mistake of exalting *means* into *ends*, or to the substitution of abstract, ethical laws and relations, for that personal Being in whom are all the springs of life.

The tendency of the human mind to the worship of abstractions, then shows itself, in *enthusiasm for the advancement of the race under the Christian ideal*, a most insidious form of the religion of abstractions, and one to which the philosophic and esthetic mind is peculiarly liable.

Noble and exalted as is such an enthusiasm, on the plane of intellectual and moral culture, it fails to rise above that plane, if it lose sight of the great end of humanity—*individual* relation, through the affections, to a personal God, from which relation of personal affection only, spring the fruits of an earnest spirituality.

That the present is a strongly Humanitarian age will not be denied.

But, while such is the character of its activity, it still contains within itself, and guards with scrupulous vigilance, those cardinal doctrines from which spring the double life of Christianity. Different sects or portions of the Church, side by side, hold each other's tendencies in check, and add each some necessary element of conservatism or progress, thus laying a broad foundation for the development of a complete Historic Christianity.

And yet everywhere, in this intellectual age, a religion of abstractions has superseded, in a great measure, that of the heart or the affections.

Christ is preached, rather as *part* of a great system by which man is rendered just with God, and the character of God justified to man, than as God Himself in History,—as a *means*, rather than as in Himself an *end*,—the supreme object of the affections; whom knowing, the Father is known, and loving, the Father is loved, and through whom alone the Father can be known and loved, for *Christology* is the only revealed *Theology*, all else bearing that name being but the product of man's reason.

A return, then, to CHRIST, to a personal, historic Christ, as the centre, head, and source of all Theology, would give to the age a vital element of progress in spirituality and true Christianity.

The grand and essential facts in the history of the Mediator, involving the destiny of man, are "as a city set upon an hill." They cannot be hid. But the foundation stones of that city are laid deep in the primeval ages of the world's history. Whoso would discover them must bring to the task something of the patience and diligence of research, the candor and fairness of spirit, which characterize the natural philosopher in his strict examination of facts in the light of their historic order and bearing.

For the student of Revelation and of Nature are but working for the same end in different departments, and should therefore be partakers of the same spirit.

They are representatives of two great classes of minds, between whom there is only a broad natural difference of *taste;* the one inclining to the consideration of *material*, and the other of *moral* phenomena.

The first class, by their diligent and accurate investigation of facts, already see unfolding before them the great laws of the material universe, and are making rapid advances in the discovery of the wisdom of God as revealed in Nature.

The other class are, in their methods of study, far behind the wisdom of the natural philosopher.

Too much like astrologers of old, shutting themselves up to their own reason or fancy, they construct a moral universe for themselves, and draw from thence deductions concerning the character and destiny of man. But Humanity can make progress only through deductions from *facts.*

A *Science of Christology*, then, or the facts of *God in Relation to Man*, consistently and progressively unfolded from early revelation, would be of vital interest to the Christian world.

Other records of Antiquity, also, or of those nations, who, wandering away from the original centre of illumination, carried with them the traditions of a primeval Christology, present a field for investigation and valuable discovery, most inviting to the Christian scholar.

The practical value of such researches at the fountain head of Pagan tradition, can hardly be estimated in their bearing upon the preaching of the Gospel to the descendants of those early wanderers.

For the Gospel is the fullness of that original Christology, whose simple, concrete facts are found floating everywhere along the turbid streams of Pagan tradition, and which, however darkened or entangled in mazes of superstition they may be, still present, in their original "ground idea," a point of contact, a *premise*, from which Revelation can be unfolded in contrast with the dark and cumbrous systems of idolatry.

An image familiar to all, found among the earliest records of Hindoo antiquity, presents itself in illustration.

The figure of Vishnoo—Preserver—is seen enfolded in the coils of the serpent who attacks his heel. Again; Vishnoo, triumphant, with elevated hands grasps the body of the serpent, and treads upon his head.

This is too exact a pictorial transcript of the promise to Eve concerning YAHVEH—the Deliverer to Come—not to suggest a close historical relationship. Here, then, is a primeval Christology in the very heart of that desperate and complicated system of Paganism, which may also be taken as representative of similar traditions existing, to some extent, in almost every form of heathen mythology.

When, through such traditions, the nations

now in darkness shall be carried back to Yahveh, the Deliverer promised to Eve, and shall behold in Christ the promised Deliverance accomplished, that day may come when "they will cast their idols of silver and of gold to the moles and the bats, and Yahveh alone shall be exalted."

Through what alternations the Church has yet to pass in its progress toward a complete Christianity, the future only can reveal.

That it will be driven into a closer personal dependence upon its Divine Leader and Saviour, no prophet's eye is needed to foresee. Already the horizon thickens with coming storms, sure to bring about this result, and to leave behind them some element of purification and vitality.

That after these storms shall have passed away, will spring forth some fairer phase of Christianity than any the world has yet seen, is not only in accordance with Prophecy, but with the facts of History.

The grand outline of the changes through which the Church must yet pass, are given in that majestic Panorama of its Progress, — The Apocalypse.

In what division of that great Pictorial Prophecy the *present* phase of the Church may be included, is perhaps not for it to know.

Inspired by the foresight of an assured victory, it should go forth "conquering, and to conquer," knowing that He, who will bring about that victory, is even now at the right hand of God, subduing all enemies under His feet.

"For he must reign till he hath put all enemies under His feet."

"Then cometh the end, when He shall nave delivered up the kingdom to God, even the Father, when He shall have put down all rule and all authority and power."

"And when all things shall be subdued unto Him, then shall the Son also Himself be subject unto Him that put all things under Him, that God may be all in all."

Thus, the Fathership of Elohim, — of that Divine Plural Personality, who in the Beginning created the heavens and the earth, — takes the place of the MEDIATORIAL RELATION after the Redeemed have entered into the inheritance of "the Sons of God,"—and ELOHIM,—from whose bosom YAHVEH ELOHIM came forth, revealing the personality of the Father, and of the Spirit,—ELOHIM—THEOS—GOD,—is at the final Ending, as at the Beginning, again,

ALL IN ALL.

FINIS.

# THEOLOGICAL SCIENCE

BY THE REV. JOHN HARRIS, D. D.

---

## THE PRE-ADAMITE EARTH: Contributions to Theological Science. New and revised edition. 12mo, cloth, 85 cts.

It opens new trains of thought; surveys the wonders of God's works, and compels Natural Science to bear her testimony in support of Divine Truth. — *Phil. Ch. Obs.*

If we do not greatly mistake, this long looked for volume will create and sustain a deep impression in the more intellectual circles of the religious world. — *Ev. Mag.*

The man who finds his element among great thoughts will read it over and over, and will find his intellect strengthened, as if from being in contact with a new creation. — *Albany Argus.*

DR. HARRIS states in a lucid, succinct, and often highly eloquent manner, all the leading facts of geology, and their beautiful harmony with the teachings of Scripture. As a work of paleontology in its relation to Scripture, it will be one of the most complete and popular extant. — *N. Y. Evangelist.*

He is a sound logician and lucid reasoner, getting nearer to the groundwork of a subject than any other writer within our knowledge. — *N. Y. Com. Advertiser.*

We have never seen the natural sciences, particularly geology, made to give so decided and unimpeachable testimony to revealed truth. The wonders of God's works, which he has here grouped together, convey a most magnificent and even overpowering idea of the Creator. We wish that we could devote a week, uninterruptedly, to its perusal and re-perusal. — *Ch. Mirror.*

Written in the glowing and eloquent style which has won for him a universal fame, and will secure a wide circle of readers. — *N. Y. Recorder.*

The elements of things, those especially that lie at the foundation of the divine relations to man, are dwelt upon in a masterly manner. — *Watchman and Reflector.*

## MAN PRIMEVAL; Or, the Constitution and Primitive Condition of the Human Being. A Contribution to Theological Science With a fine Portrait of the Author. 12mo, cloth, 1,25.

*** This is the second volume of a series of works on Theological Science. The present is a continuation of the principles of primeval nature, and are here resumed and exhibited in their next higher application to individual man.

His copious and beautiful illustrations of the successive laws of the Divine Manifestation have yielded us inexpressible delight. — *London Eclectic Review.*

In a very masterly way does our author grapple with almost every difficult and perplexing subject which comes within the range of his proposed inquiry into the constitution and condition of Man Primeval. — *London Evangelical Mag.*

Reverently recognizing the Bible as the fountain and exponent of *truth*, he is as independent and fearless as he is original and forcible; and he adds to these qualities consummate skill in argument and elegance of diction. — *N. Y. Commercial.*

DR. HARRIS has placed himself in the very front rank of scientific writers, and his essays attract the attention of the most erudite scholars of the age. — *N. Y. Observer.*

It is eminently philosophical, and at the same time glowing and eloquent. It cannot fail to have a wide circle of readers. - - *N. Y. Recorder.*

## THE FAMILY: Its Constitution, Probation, and History.

Being the third volume of the Series. *In Preparation.* Cc

# THE PREACHER AND THE KING;

OR, BOURDALOUE IN THE COURT OF LOUIS XIV.,

Being an Account of that distinguished Era. Translated from the French of L. BUNGENER. Paris, fourteenth edition. With an Introduction, by the REV. GEORGE POTTS, D. D., New York. 12mo, 1,25.

It combines *substantial history with the highest charm of romance.* We regard the book as a valuable contribution to the cause not merely of general literature, but especially of pulpit eloquence. Its attractions are so various that it can hardly fail to find readers of almost every description. — *Puritan Recorder.*

A very delightful book. It is full of interest, and equally replete with sound thought and profitable sentiment. — *N. Y. Commercial.*

It is a volume at once curious, instructive, and fascinating. Its extensive sale in France is evidence enough of its extraordinary merit and its peculiarly attractive qualities. — *Ch. Advocate.*

It is full of life and animation, and conveys a graphic idea of the state of morals and religion in the Augustan age of French literature. — *N. Y. Recorder.*

This book will attract by its novelty, and prove particularly engaging to those interested in pulpit eloquence. The author has exhibited singular skill in weaving into his narrative sketches of remarkable men, with original and striking remarks on the subject of preaching. — *Presbyterian.*

A book of rare interest, not only for the singular ability with which it is written, but for the graphic account which it gives of the state of pulpit eloquence during the celebrated era of which it treats. We warmly commend it. — *Savannah Journal.*

Its historical and biographical portions are valuable; its comments excellent, and its effect pure and benignant. — *Buffalo Morning Express.*

The author is a minister of the Reformed Church. In the forms of narrative and conversations, he portrays the features and character of that remarkable age, and illustrates the important ends to be secured by pulpit eloquence. — *Phil. Ch. Obs.*

A precious gift to the American church and ministers. It is a book full of historical facts of great value, sparkling with gems of thought, polished scholarship, and genuine piety. — *Cin. Ch. Advocate.*

This volume presents a phase of French life with which we have never met in any other work. The author is a minister of the Reformed Church in Paris, where his work has been received with unexampled popularity, having already gone through *fourteen* editions. The writer has studied not only the divinity and general literature of the age of Louis XIV., but also the *memories* of that period, until he is able to reproduce a life-like picture of society at the Court of the Grand Monarch. — *Trans.*

A work which we recommend to *all*, as possessing rare interest. — *Evening Express.*

In form it is descriptive and dramatic, presenting animated conversations between some of the most famous preachers and philosophers of the Augustan age of France. The work will be read with interest by all. The ministry cannot afford to be ignorant of the facts and suggestions of this instructive volume. — *N. Y. Ch. Intel.*

The work is very fascinating, and the lesson under its spangled robe is of the gravest moment to every pulpit and every age. — *Ch. Intelligencer.*

THE PRIEST AND THE HUGUENOT; or Persecution in the Age of Louis XV. A Sermon at Court, — A Sermon in the City, — A Sermon in the Desert. Translated from the French of L. BUNGENER, author of "The Preacher and the King." 2 vols. ☞ *A new Work.*

☞ This is truly a masterly production, full of interest, and may be set down as one of the greatest Protestant works of the age.

# UNIVERSITY SERMONS;

DELIVERED in the Chapel of Brown University. By the REV. FRANCIS WAYLAND, D. D. Third thousand. 12mo, cloth, 1,00.

☞ DR. WAYLAND has here discussed most of the prominent doctrines of the Bible in his usual clear and masterly style, viz.: Theoretical Atheism; Practical Atheism; Moral Character of Man; Love to God; Fall of Man; Justification by Works impossible; Preparation for the Advent of the Messiah; Work of the Messiah; Justification by Faith; Fall of Peter; The Church of Christ; Unity of the Church; Duty of Obedience to the Civil Magistrate; also, the Recent Revolutions in Europe.

Characterized by all that richness of thought and elegance of language for which their talented author is celebrated. — DR. BAIRD'S *Christian Union.*

The thorough logician is apparent throughout the volume, and there is a classic purity in the diction, unsurpassed by any writer, and equalled by few. — *N. Y. Com.*

One of our most popular writers in various departments of science and morals. His style is easy and fluent, and rich in illustration. — *Evangelical Review.*

No thinking man can open to any portion of it without finding his attention strongly arrested, and feeling inclined to yield his assent to those self-evincing statements which appear on every page. As a writer, Dr. Wayland is distinguished by simplicity, strength, and comprehensiveness. He addresses himself directly to the intellect, to the conscience more than to the passions. — *Watchman and Reflector.*

These discourses are fine specimens of his discriminating power of thought, and purity and vigor of style. — *Zion's Herald.*

Those who take up this volume with the high expectations induced by his previous works, will not be disappointed. The discourses are rich in evangelical truth, profound thought, and beautiful diction; worthy at once of the theologian, the philosopher, and the rhetorician. — *Albany Argus.*

This volume adds to Dr. Wayland's fame as a writer. This is commendation enough to bestow upon any book. — *Puritan Recorder.*

DR. WAYLAND is one of the most prominent Christian philosophers and literary men of our country. — *Watchman, Cincinnati.*

His style is peculiarly adapted to arrest the attention, and his familiar illustrations serve to make plain the most abstruse principles, as well as to enstamp them upon one's memory. It is, in fact, scarcely possible to forget a discourse from Wayland. We think no minister's library complete without it. — *Dover Star.*

They come from one who has attained a national reputation, and embody views matured by the study of years upon important topics in theology. — *Phil. Ch. Chron.*

## THE PERSON AND WORK OF CHRIST. By ERNEST SARTORIUS, D. D. Translated from the German, by the REV. OAKMAN S. STEARNS, A. M. 18mo, cloth, 42 cts.

A work of much ability, and presenting the argument in a style that will be new to most American readers. It will deservedly attract attention. — *N. Y. Observer.*

DR. SARTORIUS is one of the most eminent and evangelical theologians in Germany. The work will be found, both from the important subjects discussed and the earnestness, beauty, and vivacity of its style, to possess the qualities which recommend it to the Christian public. — *Mich. Ch. Herald.*

A little volume on a great subject, and evidently the production of a great mind. The style and train of thought prove this. — *Southern Literary Gazette.*

Whether we consider the importance of the subjects discussed, or the perspicuous exhibition of truth in the volume before us, or the devout spirit of the author, we cannot but desire the work an extensive circulation. — *Christian Index.* Gg

## WORKS FOR BIBLE STUDENTS.

A TREATISE ON BIBLICAL CRITICISMS; Exhibiting a Systematic View of that Science. By SAMUEL DAVIESON, D. D., of the University of Halle, Author of "Ecclesiastical Polity," "Introduction to the New Testament," etc. A new Revised and Enlarged Edition, in two elegant octavo volumes, cloth, 5,00.

These volumes contain a statement of *the sources* of criticism, such as the MSS. of the Hebrew Bible and Greek Testament, the principal versions of both, quotations from them in early writers, parallels; and also the internal evidence on which critics rely for obtaining a pure text. A history of the texts of the Old and New Testaments, with a description of the Hebrew and Greek languages in which the Scriptures are written. An examination of disputed passages. Every thing is discussed which properly belongs to *the criticism* of the text, comprehending all that comes under the title of *General Introduction* in Introductions to the Old and New Testament.

HISTORY OF PALESTINE, from the Patriarchal Age to the Present Time; with Introductory Chapters on the Geography and Natural History of the Country, and on the Customs and Institutions of the Hebrews. By JOHN KITTO, D. D., Author of "Scripture Daily Readings," "Cyclopædia of Biblical Literature," &c. With upwards of *two hundred Illustrations*. 12mo, cloth, 1,25.

A very full compendium of the geography and history of Palestine, from the earliest era mentioned in Scripture to the present day; not merely a dry record of boundaries, and the succession of rulers, but an intelligible account of the agriculture, habits of life, literature, science, and art, with the religious, political, and judicial institutions of the inhabitants of the Holy Land in all ages. A more useful and instructive book has rarely been published. — *N. Y. Commercial.*

Beyond all dispute, this is the best historical compendium of the Holy Land, from the days of Abraham to those of Mehemet Ali. — *Edinburgh Review.*

☞ In the numerous notices and reviews the work has been strongly recommended, as not only admirably adapted to the *family*, but also as a text book for *Sabbath and week day schools.*

CRUDEN'S CONDENSED CONCORDANCE; a New and Complete Concordance to the Holy Scriptures. By ALEXANDER CRUDEN. Revised and Reëdited by the Rev. DAVID KING, LL. D. Tenth Thousand. Octavo, cloth backs, 1,25.

This work is printed from English plates. and is a full and fair copy of all that is valuable as a Concordance in Cruden's larger work, in two volumes, which costs *five dollars*, while *this* edition is furnished at *one dollar and twenty-five cents!* The principal variation from the larger book consists in the exclusion of the Bible Dictionary, (which has always been an incumbrance,) the condensation of the quotations of Scripture, arranged under their most obvious heads, which, while it diminishes the bulk of the work, *greatly facilitates* the finding of any required passage.

We have, in this edition of Cruden, the *best* made better! That is, the present is better adapted to the purposes of a concordance, by the erasure of superfluous references, and the contraction of quotations, etc. It is better as a manual, and better adapted by its price, to the means of many who need and ought to possess such a work, than the former large and expensive edition. — *Puritan Recorder.*

## IMPORTANT WORK.

KITTO'S POPULAR CYCLOPÆDIA OF BIBLICAL LITERATURE. Condensed from the larger work. By the Author, JOHN KITTO, D. D., Author of "Scripture Daily Readings," &c. Assisted by JAMES TAYLOR, D. D. With *over* 500 *Illustrations*. 3,00.

This work is designed to furnish a DICTIONARY OF THE BIBLE, embodying the products of the best and most recent researches in biblical literature, in which the scholars of Europe and America have been engaged. The work, the result of immense labor and research, is pronounced, by universal consent, the best work of its class extant. It is not only intended for *ministers* and *theological students*, but is also particularly adapted to *parents, Sabbath school teachers, and the great body of the religious public*. The *illustrations*, amounting to *more than* 300, are of the highest order.

*A condensed view of the various topics comprehended in the work.*

1. BIBLICAL CRITICISM, — Embracing the History of the Bible Languages; Canon of Scripture; Literary History and Peculiarities of the Sacred Books; Formation and History of Scripture Texts.

2. HISTORY, — Proper Names of Persons; Biographical Sketches of prominent Characters; Detailed Accounts of important Events recorded in Scripture; Chronology and Genealogy of Scripture.

3. GEOGRAPHY, — Names of Places; Description of Scenery; Boundaries and Mutual Relations of the Countries mentioned in Scripture, so far as necessary to illustrate the Sacred Text.

4. ARCHÆOLOGY, — Manners and Customs of the Jews and other nations mentioned in Scripture; their Sacred Institutions, Military Affairs, Political Arrangements, Literary and Scientific Pursuits.

5. PHYSICAL SCIENCE, — Scripture Cosmogony and Astronomy, Zoology, Mineralogy, Botany, Meteorology.

In addition to numerous flattering notices and reviews, personal letters from *a large number of the most distinguished Ministers and Laymen of different religious denominations in the country* have been received, highly commending this work as admirably adapted to ministers, Sabbath school teachers, heads of families, and *all* Bible students.

The following extract of a letter is a fair specimen of individual letters received from *each* of the gentlemen whose names are given below: —

"I have examined it with special and unalloyed satisfaction. It has the rare merit of being all that it professes to be; and very few, I am sure, who may consult it will deny that, in richness and fulness of detail, it surpasses their expectation. Many ministers will find it a valuable auxiliary; but its chief excellence is, that it furnishes just the facilities which are needed by the thousands in families and Sabbath schools, who are engaged in the important business of biblical education. It is in itself a library of reliable information."

W. B. Sprague, D. D., Albany; J. J. Carruthers, D. D., Portland; Joel Hawes, D. D., Hartford, Ct.; Daniel Sharp, D. D., Boston; N. L. Frothingham, D. D., Boston; Ephraim Peabody, D. D., Boston; A. L. Stone, Boston; John S. Stone, D. D., Brooklyn; J. B. Waterbury, D. D., Boston; Baron Stow, D. D., Boston; Thomas H. Skinner, D. D., New York; Samuel W. Worcester, D. D., Salem; Horace Bushnell, D. D., Hartford, Ct.; Right Reverend J. M. Wainwright, D. D., New York; Gardner Spring, D. D., New York; W. T. Dwight, D. D., Portland; E. N. Kirk, Boston; Prof. George Bush, author of "Notes on the Scriptures," New York; Howard Malcom, D. D., author of "Bible Dictionary;" Henry J. Ripley, D. D., author of "Notes on the Scriptures;" N. Porter, Prof. in Yale College, New Haven, Ct.; Jared Sparks, Edward Everett, Theodore Frelinghuysen, Robert C. Winthrop, John McLean, Simon Greenleaf, Thomas S. Williams, — and a large number of others of like character and standing of the above, whose names cannot here appear. H

# VALUABLE WORKS.

## THE SUFFERING SAVIOUR; OR, MEDITATIONS ON THE LAST DAYS OF CHRIST.

By FRED. W. KRUMMACHER, D.D., Chaplain to the King of Prussia, and author of "Elijah the Tishbite," etc. Translated under the express sanction of the author, by SAMUEL JACKSON. 12mo, cloth. $1.25.

The style of the author need not be described to those who have read his 'Elijah; and whoever has not read an evangelical book of our own time that has passed through many editions in German, English, French, Dutch, Danish, had better order the CHINESE edition, which has recently appeared. * * * We like the book—LOVE it, rather—for the vivid perception and fervid emotion with which it brings us to the Suffering Saviour."—NEW YORK INDEPENDENT.

"Krummacher is himself again! Till the present work appeared, he had done nothing equal to his first one, 'Elijah, the Tishbite.' In the present he comes upon the literary firmament in his old fire and glory, 'like a re-appearing star.' The translator has done his work admirably. * * * Much of the narrative is given with thrilling vividness, and pathos, and beauty. Marking as we proceeded, several passages for quotation, we found them in the end so numerous, that we must refer the reader to the work itself."—NEWS OF THE CHURCHES (SCOTTISH).

## THE PROGRESS OF BAPTIST PRINCIPLES IN THE LAST HUNDRED YEARS.

By T. F. CURTIS, Professor of Theology in Lewisburg University, Pa. 12mo, cloth. $1.25.

This work is divided into three books. The first exhibits the progress of Baptist Principles, now conceeded in theory by the most enlighted of other denominations.

The second presents a view of the progress of principles still controverted.

The third sets forth the progress of principles always held by evangelical Christians, but more consistently by Baptists.

It is a work that invites the candid consideration of all denomitions. The aim has been to draw a wide distinction between parties and opinions. Hence the object of this volume is not to exhibit or defend the Baptists, but their principles."

"The principles referred to are such as these: Freedom of conscience and Separation of Church and State; a Converted Church Membership; Sacraments inoperative without Choice and Faith; Believers the only Scriptural Subjects of Baptism; Immersion always the Baptism of the New Testament; Infant Baptism Injurious; Open Communion Unwise and Injurious. To show the progress of these principles, statistics are given, from which we learn that in 1792 there was but one Baptist Communicant in the United States to every fifty-six inhabitants, while in 1854 there was one to every thirty inhabitants. The Baptists have more than one quarter of the whole Church accommodation in the United States. * * * The entire work is written with ability and unfailing good temper."—QUARTERLY JOURNAL AMERICAN UNITARIAN ASSOCIATION.

"The good temper of the author of this volume is obvious; the method of arranging his materials for effect admirable."—PRESBYTERIAN.

"We know of no man in our Churches better fitted to prepare a fair exhibition of 'Baptist Principles.' He is no controversialist; and his discussions are in most refreshing contrast with many, both of Baptist defenders and their opponents."—SOUTHERN BAPTIST.

"The work exhibits ample learning, vigorous argumentative power, and an excellent spirit toward those whose views it controverts. Apart from its theological bearings, it possesses not a little historical interest."—N. Y. TRIBUNE.

"The aim of the work is important, the plan ingenious, yet simple and natural, the author's preparation for it apparently thorough and conscientious, and his spirit excellent."—WATCHMAN AND REFLECTOR.

# MIALL'S WORKS.

FOOTSTEPS OF OUR FOREFATHERS; what they Suffered and what they Sought. Describing Localities and portraying Personages and Events conspicuous in the Struggles for Religious Liberty. By JAMES G. MIALL. Thirty-six fine Illustrations. 12mo, 1,00.

An exceedingly entertaining work. It is full of strong points. The reader soon catches the fire and zeal of those sterling men whom we have so long admired, and ere he is aware becomes so deeply enlisted in their cause that he finds it difficult to lay aside the book till finished. — *Ch. Parlor Mag.*

A book to stir one's spirit to activity and self-sacrifice in the work of God. It portrays the character, deeds, sufferings, and the success of those heroic non-conformists who stood up for the truth. It is a book worthy of a large sale. — *Zion's Herald.*

A work absorbingly interesting, and very instructive. — *Western Lit. Magazine.*

The title attracted our attention; its contents have held us fast to its pages to the very close. It is full of antiquarian lore and abounds in charming local descriptions. — *Watchman and Reflector.*

The events narrated and scenes described give us impressive views of the great sacrifices made by the noble sufferers for the priceless boon of spiritual freedom. — *Ch. Observer.*

Biographical notices of those noble minds who made the grand discoveries of civil and religious liberty in England. The anecdotes of these men and their times are full of interest, and are drawn from the most authentic sources. — *Nat. Intel.*

This is a most captivating book, and one that the reader is compelled to finish if he once begins it. We really wish that every family in our land could have a copy. It has kept us perfectly enchained from beginning to end. — *Newport Observer.*

MEMORIALS OF EARLY CHRISTIANITY; Presenting, in graphic and popular Form, Memorable Events of Early Ecclesiastical History, etc. By JAMES G. MIALL. Illustrations. 12mo, cloth, 1,00.

☞ This, like the "Footsteps of our Forefathers," is a work of uncommon interest.

We thank Mr. Miall for this volume. There are plain truths plainly told in this volume about ancient Christianity and the practices of the Christians of ante-Nicene times which we could wish *churchmen* would lay to heart and profit by. —*Epis. Reg.*

More interesting than a *romance*, and yet full of instruction. — *Hartford Times.*

A work of no ordinary value, and we commend it to all. Every Sabbath school should be supplied with copies. — *Ch. Secretary.*

Mr. Miall is a Congregational minister in England, and a popular writer of unusual power. He has the power of graphic delineation, and has given us pictures of early Christianity which have the charm of life and reality. Our readers are assured that its glowing pages will excite their admiration. — *N. Y. Recorder.*

This is an extremely interesting work, embodying classic and ecclesiastic lore, and calculated to do much good by bringing the church of *to-day* into closer acquaintanceship and sympathy with the church of the early past. — *Congregationalist.*

The *results* of extended research are offered to the general reader in a style of *uncommon* interest.— *Watchman and Reflector.*

We have in an attractive form some of the most important facts of early ecclesiastical history, in illustration of the purity and power of Christian faith. — *Puritan Rec.*

A volume of thrilling interest. It takes the reader through a very important period of secular and ecclesiastical history. — *Western Lit. Messenger.*

Yy

# IMPORTANT NEW WORKS.

---

## THE CHRISTIAN LIFE: Social and Individual. By Peter Bayne, A. M. 12mo, cloth. $1.25.

**Contents.** Part I. — Statement. The Individual Life; the Social Life. Part II. — Exposition and Illustration. First Principles; Howard, and the rise of Philanthropy; Wilberforce, and the development of Philanthropy; Budgett, the Christian Freeman; the social problem of the age, and one or two hints towards its solution; Modern Doubt; John Foster; Thomas Arnold; Thomas Chalmers. Part III. — Outlook. The Positive Philosophy; Pantheistic Spiritualism.

Particular attention is invited to this work. Its recent publication in Scotland produced a great sensation. Hugh Miller made it the subject of an elaborate review in his paper, the Edinburgh "Witness," and gave his readers to understand that it was an extraordinary work. The "News of the Churches," the monthly organ of the Scottish Free Church, was equally emphatic in its praise, pronouncing it "the religious book of the season." Strikingly original in plan and brilliant in execution, it far surpasses the expectations raised by the somewhat familiar title. It is, in truth, a bold onslaught (and the first of the kind) upon the Pantheism of Carlyle, Fichte, etc., by an ardent admirer of Carlyle; and at the same time an exhibition of the Christian Life, in its inner principle, and as illustrated in the lives of Howard, Wilberforce, Budgett, Foster, Chalmers, etc. The brilliancy and vigor of the author's style are remarkable.

## PATRIARCHY; or, The Family: its Constitution and Probation. By John Harris, D. D., President of "New College," London, and author of "The Great Teacher," "Mammon," etc. 12mo, cloth. $1.25.

The public are here presented with a work on a subject of universal interest, by one of the most able and popular living authors. It is a work that should find a place in every family, containing, as it does, a profound and eloquent exposition of the constitution, laws, and history of the Family, as well as much important instruction and sound advice, touching the family, family government, family education, etc., of the present time.

This is the third and last of a series, by the same author, entitled "Contributions to Theological Science." The plan of this series is highly original, and thus far has been most successfully executed. Of the first two in the series, "Pre-Adamite Earth," and "Man Primeval," we have already issued four and five editions, and the demand still continues. The immense sale of all Dr. Harris's works attest their intrinsic popularity.

"The present age has not produced his superior as an original, stirring, elegant writer." — Philadelphia Christian Chronicle.

## GOD REVEALED IN NATURE AND IN CHRIST; Including a Refutation of the Development Theory contained in the "Vestiges of the Natural History of Creation." By the author of "The Philosophy of the Plan of Salvation." 12mo, cloth. $1.25.

The author of that remarkable book, "The Philosophy of the Plan of Salvation," has devoted several years of incessant labor to the preparation of this work. It furnishes a new, and, as it is conceived, a conclusive argument against the "development theory" so ingeniously maintained in the "Vestiges of the Natural History of Creation." As this author does not publish except when he has something to say, there is good reason to anticipate that the work will be one of unusual interest and value. His former book has met with the most signal success in both hemispheres, having passed through numerous editions in England and Scotland, and been translated into four of the European languages besides. It is also about to be translated into the Hindostanee tongue.

www.ingramcontent.com/pod-product-compliance
Lightning Source LLC
LaVergne TN
LVHW011227110826
845150LV00006B/1568
*9781425515980*